FOR JOHN
WITH THANKS FOR
STANDING BEHIND ME
— AND SAYING I SHOULD
GET A BOOK OUT!
        WITH WARMEST AFFECTION,

EVIL AND THE UNCONSCIOUS

ÆR

American Academy of Religion
Studies in Religion

James O. Duke, Editor

Number 30
EVIL AND THE UNCONSCIOUS
by
Walter Lowe

EVIL AND THE UNCONSCIOUS

WALTER LOWE

Scholars Press
Chico, California

EVIL AND THE UNCONSCIOUS

by
Walter Lowe

Library of Congress Cataloging in Publication Data

Lowe, Walter, 1940-.
    Evil and the unconscious.

    (Studies in religion / American Academy of Religion ;
no. 30)
    Includes bibliographical references.
    1. Psychoanalysis. 2. Good and evil. 3. Subconsciousness.
4. Humanistic psychology. 5. Humanism. I. Title. II. Series:
Studies in religion (American Academy of Religion) ; no. 30.
BF175.L685 1983   150.19   82-19147
ISBN 0-89130-600-5

Printed in the United States of America

For Barbara—

joy and gratitude

Table of Contents

If we are unaware of just how far necessity and a fickle fortune hold the human soul under their domination, we cannot treat as our equals nor love as ourselves those whom chance has separated from us by an abyss. The diversity of the constraints to which humankind is subject creates the illusion that there are different species among us which cannot communicate with one another. Only those who have known the empire of might and yet have not bowed down before it are capable of justice and love.

Simone Weil
translation adapted from *The Simone Weil Reader*

PREFACE

Since the 1960s the thought of Sigmund Freud, long dismissed as an out-moded reductionism, has been the subject of a remarkable philosophic discussion in Europe. The impetus for this collective "return to Freud" has come from a series of groundbreaking interpretations of the unconscious, variously set forth by Jacques Lacan, Paul Ricoeur, Jürgen Habermas, and Jacques Derrida.[1] The emerging view of Freud, while many-faceted and much disputed, shows promise of leading us out of the reductionist wasteland. But it also has the effect, which has been somewhat less remarked, of dramatically underscoring the extent to which the human condition is marked by tragic conflict and self-delusion. It is this latter aspect which the present essays seek particularly to explore, with a view toward the concerns of theology.

To talk about the problem of evil—even to call it a "problem"—must raise suspicions that one is only talking, that the matter is not being taken seriously. At the same time, when evil is made the center of attention, when it appears in the title of a book, one must wonder whether the case is not being *over*stated: whether the human prospect is not being belittled in order to prepare the way, perhaps, for a covert theological agenda. These cautions have accompanied me throughout the writing of the present essays, and I have attended to them as best I can. Yet I have also come to feel that insofar as they lead to an argument over pessimism and optimism—is the picture too bleak? is it not bleak enough?—the questions themselves may be misleading. Surely our initiation into this issue must amount to something more than a debate over the chromatics of evil.

Indeed, focusing upon that question may be a way of keeping the real task at arm's length. It is a little like trying to say at the beginning of psychotherapy, before one has entered into the therapeutic process, just what one's problems are and how deep they go. In therapy as in the present discussion, I believe, one simply cannot know at the outset what all one is

---

[1] See Jacques Lacan, *Écrits* (Paris: Editions du Seuil, 1966); Stuart Schneiderman, ed. and trans., *Returning to Freud: Clinical Psychoanalysis in the School of Lacan* (New Haven: Yale University Press, 1980); John P. Muller and William J. Richardson, eds., *Lacan Interpreted: A Reader's Guide to Selected Texts* (New York: International Universities Press, 1980); Paul Ricoeur, *Freud and Philosophy: An Essay on Interpretation*, trans. Denis Savage (New Haven: Yale University Press, 1970); Jürgen Habermas, *Knowledge and Human Interests*, trans. Jeremy J. Shapiro (Boston: Beacon Press, 1971); Jacques Derrida, *Writing and Difference*, trans. Alan Bass (Chicago: University of Chicago Press, 1978); idem, *Of Grammatology*, trans. Gayatri Spivak (Baltimore: Johns Hopkins University Press, 1976).

getting into. One takes the chance and finds out as one goes along. And, all
allowances made for the differences, the reasons are similar in the one case
and in the other. They have to do with our tendency to hold fast to our
illusions, be they great or small, and to avoid the arduous process of working through. Disillusion which is defined in advance brings no insight
because it requires no relinquishment. Once again, we cannot know in
advance what form this letting go may take, or whether its demands will be
great or slight. But relinquishment there must be, if we are ever to find out
what may be on the other side.[2] For as Philip Slater observes, "without
despair we cannot transfer our allegiance to reality—it is a kind of mourn-
ing period for our fantasies."[3]

The book is therefore an extended effort to take with full seriousness the
Freudian form of what Ricoeur has called "the hermeneutic of suspicion."
For me it was Ricoeur who initially set the terms for such an effort, and
time and again I return to Ricoeur as a way of touching ground.[4] But grad-
ually in the course of writing the essays I grew dissatisfied with Ricoeur's
position, and in trying to give voice to my reservations I found myself
turning increasingly to the Frankfurt School of critical theory. The
influence of Theodor Adorno, in particular, has been for me far more pervasive than the occasional references may suggest.[5] But behind the Frankfurt
School stands Hegel; and in many respects, for better and for worse, it is
with Hegel that we must come to terms.[6] It is instructive, for example, that
in writing the Preface to *The Phenomenology of Spirit* Hegel found it necessary
to position himself not only against a shallow empiricism—that target was
obvious enough—but against the formless enthusiasm of an "indeterminate"
romanticism as well. "Just as there is an empty breadth," he cautioned, "so
too there is an empty depth."[7]

With this recognition as with many, Hegel remains our contemporary.
Empty depth has recently become a hot commodity on the cultural market.
The same period which saw a return to Freud in Europe has witnessed, on a
popular level in the United States, the widespread acceptance of the "human

[2] The analogy with therapy is developed further in Walter Lowe, "Method between Two
Disciplines: The Therapeutic Analogy," *The Journal of Pastoral Care* 35, no. 3, (September
1981): 147–56.

[3] Philip Slater, *Earthwalk* (Garden City, NY: Anchor Press, Doubleday, 1974), p. 2.

[4] See particularly Paul Ricoeur, *The Conflict of Interpretations: Essays in Hermeneutics* (Evanston: Northwestern University Press, 1974), pp. 440–67.

[5] A. Arato and F. Gebhardt, eds., *The Essential Frankfurt School Reader* (New York: Urizen
Books, 1978); Theodor Adorno, *Negative Dialectics* (New York: Seabury Press, 1973); Gillian
Rose, *The Melancholy Science: An Introduction to the Thought of Theodor W. Adorno* (New York:
Columbia University Press, 1978).

[6] Cf. the remarkably appreciative assessment of Hegel in Karl Barth, *Protestant Theology in
the Nineteenth Century: Its Background and History* (Valley Forge: Judson Press, 1973), pp. 409–21.

[7] G. W. F. Hegel, *Phenomenology of Spirit*, trans. A. V. Miller (Oxford: Clarendon Press,
1977), p. 6.

potential movement." In and through its great variety, the movement is characterized by an open-ended optimism about the possibilities of human growth and, not coincidentally, a cool disdain for the psychology of Freud.[8] This striking cultural contrast between this country and Europe is hardly accidental; the popular psychologies of the sixties and seventies, while they run counter to much of contemporary experience, still fit hand-in-glove with convictions of progress and promise which are deeply ingrained in the American spirit. A fit which is so natural remains largely unreflective, and without strenuous reflection we continue to float on the surface of psyche and society. In a familiar passage Hegel warned against "the night in which all cows are black."[9] It is not clear that we have scored an unambiguous gain when, alternatively, the world has been suffused with unrelieved sunshine.

The essays thus circle about a set of common concerns; but they proceed quite variously. "Psychoanalysis as an Archaeology of Suffering" sets forth in brief, almost telegraphic fashion some of the recurrent themes of the book. If allowances are made for its somewhat polemical character, it is perhaps the most accessible point at which to begin. "Beyond Humanistic Psychology," in contrast, develops its argument inductively, showing in some detail how the critique initiated by some of the best commentators on Freud and theology might be further developed and clarified. Ricoeur is among these commentators; I argue that he has opened new dimensions in the reading of Freud but that he seems almost willfully determined not to follow through on his own discoveries. This puzzling hesitancy seems to me symptomatic of a chronic problem within the field, and so in the following chapter I try to determine its sources. The conclusion I draw is that Ricoeur's holding back may be ascribed, in large part, to his understanding of the reponsibilities of a Christian humanism.

"Humanism" in this broad sense is by no means interchangeable with humanistic psychology, but there are certain perspectives, particularly the Freudian, from which the two have much in common. The critical interplay among these perspectives is the subject of chapter 3. The essay contains a more balanced appreciation of humanistic psychology, as well as the fullest statement of the book's somewhat ad hoc methodology.

Chapter 4, the title essay, seeks to recapture Freud's view of the human condition. It begins from within the perspective of two American commentators, examines the thematics of tragedy and self-delusion and arrives at a position which is indebted to Jacques Lacan. Finally, the essay on "Innocence and Experience" was written to serve as the theological contribution to a collective volume on *Psychoanalysis and the Problem of Evil*, to be read

---

[8] Anthony J. Sutich and Miles A. Vich, eds., *Readings in Humanistic Psychology* (New York: The Free Press, 1969); H. Newton Maloney, ed., *Current Perspectives in the Psychology of Religion* (Grand Rapids: Eerdmans, 1977).

[9] Hegel, *Phenomenology of Spirit*, p. 9.

primarily by analysts. The discussion thus begins with a broad, introductory typology of Western views of the problem of evil. It then examines Tillich and Jung as a way of opening up certain issues which lead, in the concluding sections, to a revised understanding of the Western debate.

In preparing the essays for this volume I have made minor revisions of substance and style. While I have sought to minimize duplication, a certain amount of repetition has seemed necessary in order to enable each essay to stand more or less on its own. For similar reasons, the notes to each chapter have been made to be self-contained. It should now be possible to approach the chapters in whatever order one desires; some readers may well find that, after the Introduction, the later, more general chapters are the better place to begin.

This volume owes many debts which it is a pleasure to recall. To the warm collegiality of the faculty of the Candler School of Theology, and especially to Dean Jim Waits for assistance in freeing time to pursue this research. To the members of the AAR Work Group on Psycho-Social Interpretations in Theology, and of the Work Group on Constructive Christian Theology which met annually at Vanderbilt University and at the Institute for Ecumenical and Cultural Research in Collegeville, Minnesota. To the American Council of Learned Societies for a grant, under a program funded by the National Endowment for the Humanities, which provided support for the final preparation of the manuscript. To Walter Adamson, Edward Casey, Michael Eigen and Rodney Hunter for hours of sage counsel and encouragement. To James Duke for his able editorial assistance. And to Sharyn Scales and Michael Bohannon for the care and unfailing good humor which they brought to the tasks of typing and preparing the manuscript.

Finally, this book is dedicated to my wife, Barbara DeConcini, whose participation has been so important to these essays from first conversation to final proofing, and whose companionship during these years has taught me so much about the meaning of memory and celebration.

ACKNOWLEDGMENTS

"Psychoanalysis as an Archaeology of the History of Suffering," reprinted, with permission, from *Concilium* 156, *The Challenge of Psychology to Faith*, ed. Steven Kepnes and David Tracy (1982), published by Seabury Press, New York.

"Beyond Humanistic Psychology," reprinted, with permission, from *Religious Studies Review* 4, no. 4 (October 1978): 246-54, published by the Council on the Study of Religion, Wilfred Laurier University, Waterloo, Ontario.

"The Coherence of Paul Ricoeur," reprinted, with permission, from *The Journal of Religion* 61, no. 4 (1981): 384-402, published by the University of Chicago Press, Chicago. Copyright 1981 by The University of Chicago. All rights reserved. 0022-4189/81/6104-0003.

"Psychoanalysis and Humanism: The Permutations of Method," reprinted, with permission, from the *Journal of the American Academy of Religion* 47, 1 Supplement (March 1979): 135-69, published by the American Academy of Religion. Reprinted in *Proceedings of the Thirty-Fourth Annual Convention of the Catholic Theological Society of America* 34, ed. Luke Salm (1979-80): 99-122.

"Evil and the Unconscious: A Freudian Exploration," reprinted, with permission, from *Soundings* 63, no. 1 (Spring 1980): 7-35. Copyright 1980 by the Society for Values in Higher Education and Vanderbilt University.

"Innocence and Experience: The Historical Dimensions of the Problem of Evil," reprinted, with permission, from *Psychoanalysis and the Concept of Evil*, ed. Marie Coleman Nelson and Michael Eigen (New York: Human Sciences Press, 1982).

INTRODUCTION
PSYCHOANALYSIS AS AN ARCHAEOLOGY
OF SUFFERING

In psychoanalysis nothing is
true except the exaggerations.
Theodor Adorno

"Drive," "instinct," "impulse," "repression." The challenge of psychology to theology would not seem far to seek. In the very language of psychoanalysis it presses itself upon us. Throughout the classic Freudian texts a bizarre vocabulary of drive and impulse, force and counterforce, evokes the fantastic image of a sort of psychic plumbing system, a sexual hydraulics of the mind! The proposal's sheer effrontery, the more offensive for being espoused in the name of science, has long drawn upon psychoanalysis the wrath of theology. For almost as long, theology's task has seemed self-evident: to allow Freud his limited truth, to refute his fundamental reductionism, and then to fish about for a more adequate psychology.

But there is another side of psychoanalysis which finds no place in the conventional critique. It has to do with the actual practice of analysis, but it is not just the concession that analysis may be of therapeutic value. It is the fact that in its practice analysis manifests a very specific concern for the recovery of traumatic memories—for *the recollection of suffering*. Christian reflection, for its part, has only recently become clear about the importance of the memory of suffering for a faithful and critical theology. "As the remembered history of suffering," J. B. Metz observes, "history retains the form of 'dangerous tradition.'"[1] Here are neglected resources for dialogue. Theology could learn more concretely the nature of such memory and means of access to it. Psychoanalysis could be instructed on the significance of its work.

It is at just this point of great promise, however, that the discussion gets derailed. For the analyst holds that the memories are not just forgotten, they have been actively repressed; whence it follows that to understand how they came to be repressed and how they may yet be retrieved, one must draw

---

[1] Johannes B. Metz, *Faith in History and Society: Toward a Practical Fundamental Theology*, trans. David Smith (New York: Seabury Press, 1979), p. 110. This volume came into my hands as I was completing the present essays. I would wish to ally myself with many of Metz's arguments.

upon concepts of psychological force and counterforce. But that is the very language the theologians have been most anxious to expunge. For Freud, according to the common argument, was rather like Columbus. He discovered a new world, and all honor to him for that; but when he set about describing his discovery, he fell victim to certain inherited preconceptions. He imposed upon the human psyche the language of a mechanistic physics which was the paradigmatic science of his day.[2]

The psychological challenge, on this account, is twofold and clear-cut: positively, to appropriate Freud's therapeutic gains; negatively, to critique his reductionistic theory. The present essay intends to deny neither of these tasks, but only the claim to exhaustiveness. For there is a third challenge which is not so readily categorized. It concerns the psychoanalytic treatment of memory, which is closely associated with the distrusted language of force, and which yet, as the recollection of suffering, holds great promise for theology. To make this clear requires a recovery of psychoanalysis as a mode of critical thinking. To prepare the way for such a recovery I shall first examine some difficulties which have arisen within the traditional responses to Freud, where the critique of reductionism has tended to be the overriding concern. Then I shall offer some constructive proposals.

THE ISSUE OF REDUCTIONISM

The various responses to Freud by theology, and by the humanities at large, may be surveyed in terms of a simple typology. Let us distinguish an early hermeneutical, an existentialist and a late hermeneutical response.

1. Early hermeneutical response

This is perhaps the most straightforward position. It turns upon Wilhelm Dilthey's classic distinction between *Erklären* and *Verstehen*, explanation and understanding. The former, which proceeds in terms of cause and effect, is the trademark of the natural sciences. But the *Geisteswissenschaften*, the human sciences, require a quite different discourse which is no less legitimate, one bearing reference to human purpose and meaning. This distinction, by which Dilthey sought to establish the human sciences on an equal footing with the natural sciences, continues to the present day in various proposals for a holistic or humanistic psychology. Now Dilthey was aware that the distinction should not be made too sharply; yet this is exactly what happened in a number of antireductionist arguments. Moreover, certain powerful value terms such as "inner life" and "meaning" tended to be located on one side of the distinction. But if human meaning is

---

[2] If Hans Küng's recent book departs from this timeworn pattern in any significant way, I am unable to detect it. See Hans Küng, *Freud and the Problem of God*, trans. Edward Quinn (New Haven: Yale University Press, 1979).

the prerogative of the human sciences, then by implication the natural sciences are finally meaningless. The suggestion is seductive, especially when not fully explicit; but it scarcely has a holistic, integrative effect. The result is apparent in the divided mind of current popular psychology, where an unresolved and largely unacknowledged contradiction exists between the humanistic psychologies which stress the distinctively human (be it meaning, creativity or what have you) and the holistic psychologies, which hold that the modern preoccupation with human distinctiveness must give way to a participatory immersion in the body, in nature, in the universal whole.

2. Existentialist response

With the existentialists the perplexities of the earlier position become transformed into a positive and explicit program. Meaning and purpose are unambiguously placed to one side of the human equation. To the other side lies scientific causal explanation, which may distract us from the human reality: it is secondary at best and often suspect. For the Sartre of *Being and Nothingness*, the Freudian psychology amounts to a willful self-delusion, an exercise in bad faith. But the problem cast out the front door by a radical clarification returns quietly through the back. For in much of existentialism it is argued that human existence is constituted by a fundamental paradox, namely the fact that we are both finite and free. To neglect *either* pole, transcendence *or* facticity, cuts the nerve of our very existence; it entails a self-delusion which some theologians have equated with sin. And yet, this caution notwithstanding, there is in existentialism, as in the earlier position, an undeniable tendency to place the value terms to one side of the crucial distinction. It is no accident that existentialism is known specifically as a philosophy of freedom; for it is freedom the position asserts, in the face of all who would deny or reduce it. Thus the importance attached to the openness of the future as opposed to the fixity of the past, the realm of facticity. This unstinting advocacy of freedom is meant to critique the scientific reductionist; yet in the end it bids fair to be reductionist itself: reductionist in the opposite direction, as it were, in light of the existentialist's own more considered pronouncements about irreducible polarity. One may wonder whether Freud may not have something to say which the existentialists ought in principle to have recognized, but which has escaped the existential psychology.[3]

3. Late hermeneutical response

This question brings us to the late hermeneutical position, which we shall consider at somewhat greater length. Like the existentialists, Paul

---

[3] A fuller discussion would treat the manner in which a more complex figure such as Heidegger may transcend this paradigm.

Ricoeur undertakes a philosophy of the human subject. But existentialism tends to make appeal to introspective intuition, a procedure which, on Ricoeur's view, risks a narcissistic self-absorption. Thus Ricoeur prefers to approach the human subject indirectly, by way of the cultural texts in which subjectivity has been objectified. The return to hermeneutics is prompted, in other words, by a desire to purify our fallible self-understanding. Hermeneutics becomes a means toward a critical comprehension of the self.

But if it is true of hermeneutics in general that the objectivity of the texts is a way of getting us outside ourselves, then might not the same be true a fortiori of the study of a text such as Freud's, which is so very resistant to our common sense? Might not there be something even in Freud's mechanistic metaphors which bears the seeds not of an alien objectivism, but of a liberating objectivity? That is the wager which undergirds Ricoeur's massive study of Freud. Ricoeur says of Freud's peculiar vocabulary, which mixes with such insouciance the two types of discourse which Dilthey labored to disentangle, "I hope to show that there are good reasons for this apparent ambiguity, that this mixed discourse is the raison d'être of psychoanalysis."[4] This proposal marks a fundamental advance. It suggests, in a manner not previously possible, that Freud's language is not simply a product of confusion, a category mistake, but that it is a positive achievement to be confronted and worked through. The implication is that it would be misguided to conceive of the Freudian legacy solely in reductionist terms, i.e., as consisting solely of the language of force; and that it would be *equally* distorting to translate Freud exhaustively into *revisionist* terms, i.e., into the language of meaning.

Ricoeur supports his premise by noting that the realm in which psychoanalysis operates is at language's remote lower boundary, where inchoate desire struggles to gain expression. "What makes desire the limit concept at the frontier between the organic and the psychical is the fact that desire is both the nonspoken and the wish-to-speak, the unnameable and the potency to speak."[5] Thus Freud's anomalous language may perhaps be justified in that it corresponds, in some still ill-defined way, to the boundary at which the analyst works.

For us mortals, living within language as we do, that boundary is a sort of horizon. It is a limit; and because a limit, it is the place where illusion most readily appears. We imagine that this or that desired object may be the realization of all our dreams. We confuse object and horizon, the instance and the desire; it is a sort of idolatry. Thus the task of therapy is in effect to

---

[4] Paul Ricoeur, *Freud and Philosophy: An Essay on Interpretation*, trans. Denis Savage (New Haven: Yale University Press, 1970), p. 65.

[5] Ibid., p. 457. Ricoeur's phrase "the wish-to-speak" plays upon the French idiom *vouloir dire*, "to mean."

recover the distinction between the two, relativizing the object against the limitless horizon, the ever-receding expanse. There is to therapy, then, this perpetual, critical task of learning to live with limits, including the limits imposed by the very boundlessness of desire.

But Ricoeur goes on to postulate an upper horizon as well. For just as our language is rooted in desire, it is simultaneously able to transcend itself in the direction of ideal sense. This is the direction attested by Hegel; and Ricoeur displays great subtlety in arguing for an irreducible dialectic or interplay between the Freudian "archaeology" (e.g., the digging back into what is past and repressed) and the Hegelian teleology. As his study draws to a close, however, there emerges from this interaction a *second*, larger sense of "teleology" which gathers up both archaeology and the earlier teleology. That this is not the advance it might seem is evident in the very notion of horizon, which declines from being possibility-and-limit to being primarily possibility, to the detriment of its role as critical limit. And if, disturbed by this turn of events, one then returns to Ricoeur's textual analysis of Freud, one finds the vast preponderance of argument is devoted to showing that the language of force never appears in isolation, but is always related to the language of meaning. Almost entirely lacking is any equally emphatic exposition as to why the language of force is there in the first place, or why it should be retained.[6]

4. A preliminary assessment

We may conclude that while it has contributed much, the late hermeneutical position succumbs at last to a difficulty not unlike that observed in the previous two. Again certain distinctions have been made, again the integrity of each side has been affirmed: on one level, the significance of the two languages; on another level, the mutual irreducibility of archaeology and teleology. And yet again a premium has been placed on one side to the detriment of the other; indeed to the detriment of the entire dialectic.

How is one to account for this recurrent bias, this pattern of diminishment in even the most discerning responses to Freud? Adorno provides a clue when he cautions that "in the history of philosophy we repeatedly find epistemological categories turned into moral ones."[7] That is precisely the turn that is taken, to a greater or lesser extent, in each of the foregoing positions. The transformation serves to advertise the discussion's human significance; one knows that human welfare is at stake. But there is an unintended side effect as well. For once the discussion is cast in moral

---

[6] For an analogous critique of Jürgen Habermas, the other major representative of the late hermeneutical position, see Russell Keat, *The Politics of Social Theory: Habermas, Freud, and the Critique of Positivism* (Chicago: University of Chicago Press, 1981).

[7] Theodor Adorno, *Negative Dialectics,* trans. E. B. Ashton (New York: Seabury Press, 1973), p. 35.

terms, it becomes increasingly difficult for the "lower" categories, such as the language of force or the archaeology, to compete with the "higher" for their fair share of that moral weight. Moreover, when the moral note is actively stressed, as occurs when the critique of reductionism becomes the overriding concern, it may readily seem that the "higher" is in need of protection—and that it is the "lower" itself which poses the threat. The result is an imbalance, a skewing of the ongoing discussion, which makes itself felt in even so judicious a treatment as the Ricoeurian hermeneutic.

Yet to return to a clean disengagement of the moral from the epistemological is not a possibility; for reductionism does require attention and moral issues are indeed at stake. The way forward, instead, is to insist that if moral significance is to be ascribed to the one set of terms, then it must be ascribed with equal insistence to the other set as well. And that is the question before us—can we discern an inherent moral significance in the Freudian "archaeology," and in the language of force?

THE ARCHAEOLOGY OF SUFFERING

From time to time when I visit the local bookstore, I pace off the six-tiered section of shelves devoted to popular psychology, transpersonal psychology, parapsychology, astrology of personality, self-help and self-improvement. Recently it has been running around thirty-four feet. This seemingly endless stream of literature is reflective of the fact that middle-class American culture, and the middle-class church along with it, has for years been awash in a vague but congenial optimism about the vistas of human potential. This sense of limitless possibility is sponsored by a sort of psychology; and whatever that psychology is, it is *not* reductionistic—not in the usual sense of the word. It affirms religion, it affirms the human; there is little it will not affirm. But what it affirms it swallows up, while itself remaining formless. It is lacking in the prophetic, it is lacking in the critical. It is, to adapt a phrase from T. E. Hulme, psychology as spilt religion.

One reason this thing has become so rampant is that it has caught us on our theological blind side. One can of course object that in certain of its procedures it tries to manipulate God; but the various disciples will readily respond, "Oh no, we are *against* manipulation!" Beyond that minimal exchange, the traditional theological response seems to have little resource with which to mount a critique of this amiable psychology. It becomes apparent, in retrospect, that we have labored to construct a theological Maginot line. Our conceptual artillery, fixed as it was in the direction of the reductionists, was incapable of readjusting when a different psychology swept upon us from another direction. And soon it no longer mattered; the church's critical faculties had been overwhelmed in a warm, viscous flood of affirmation.

I exaggerate a little, perhaps, but only to draw attention to a very real phenomenon. It is the cultural embodiment of the conceptual bias which was traced in the previous section. It makes palpable the need for a more evenhanded approach: one which can grasp the critical import of the very aspect of psychoanalysis most readily dismissed by the antireductionist argument and by the popular psychologies.

1. The language of force

Nothing is more central to the practice of analysis than the phenomenon of transference, the powerful interpersonal relationship generated between client and therapist which provides the crucial leverage for dealing with the client's resistances. It is a matter of debate the extent to which the relationship requires of the therapist an empathetic response to the client's needs. But there is agreement that, whatever else, the therapist must maintain a considerable measure of detachment. The therapist must never cease to regard the dynamics of transference with a canny, analytic eye; for she is constantly drawing upon the interpersonal dynamic, channeling it in such a way as to further the emergent therapeutic goal. But this is in effect to say that the therapist *uses* the relationship: the therapist treats the I-Thou as an It![8]

What could possibly justify such a procedure? Either it is grounds for rejecting psychoanalysis out of hand—or it is evidence of how serious the problem is. On the latter premise, the tactical objectification which occurs in analytic practice may be viewed as a measure necessitated by a certain objectification, a certain reification, which has occurred within the individual. The human past may be conceived as the cumulative result of a constant process of sedimentation. Where there has been pain, the very memory may harden and contract, like a scar forming over a wound. The injury is then borne into the present in such patterns of behavior as obsession and hysteria. But whatever the form it may take, there is to such injury a common, identifying trait: that the individual has become less free, more constrained—in a real sense, more mechanical.

But mightn't this phenomenon be related, then, to Freud's mechanistic language? Much of the language, no doubt, is straightforwardly naturalistic and must be accepted or rejected as such. But mightn't it also refer in part to "*second* nature": that is, to the acquired but long-established set of habits and mannerisms, quirks and vulnerabilities, which are ingrained in one's character? In that case the reference would not simply be to some ultimate substrate of animality, the source of unreflective impulse, but to the *interaction* of impulse, decision and circumstance, and to the complex layering

---

[8] For an introductory discussion of transference and resistance in the therapeutic process, see Bill L. Kell and William J. Mueller, *Impact and Change: A Study of Counseling Relationships* (New York: Appleton-Century-Crofts, 1966); cf. James E. Dittes, *The Church in the Way* (New York: Scribner's, 1967), pp. 136–85 and *passim*.

which results—in short, to the individual *histories* which make us what we are.[9]

2. Discerning the challenges

This interpretation of Freud has definite antireductionist implications, which become clear the moment one stresses, as we have done, that even his most mechanistic language refers not simply to some isolated instinctual nature, but also to history. One may draw the conclusion that even at his most deterministic, Freud tacitly acknowledged the role of human freedom. The argument would be much like Ricoeur's, when he shows that the language of force is never entirely detached from a correlative language of sense.

But stressing the note of freedom diverts attention from one decisive fact, namely that we are dealing not with history in some generalized sense, but quite specifically with the history *of suffering*. It further obscures the fact, which has already been sufficiently obscured, that this is a history which has been assiduously denied, impacted and forgotten; and that often all we have left by which to recover it are the omissions and tics, the distortions and scars—precisely the marks of *un*freedom—which that history has bequeathed us.

Now if this distinctive face of psychoanalysis does pose its own distinctive challenge to theology—a challenge of theodicy, a challenge to keep faith with the history of suffering as it presents itself in this humble psychological guise—it is not a challenge which can be ranged unreflectively alongside the previous two. For there exists between the present concern and the previously recognized tasks of appropriating therapeutic benefit and critiquing reductionist theory, a substantial conceptual tension. Thus in the case just noted, the antireductionist preoccupation with the reality of freedom inevitably diverted attention from the archaeological effort to patiently, methodically bring to light the intricate network of human caughtness.

The point may be put more emphatically. It must be said that a true word spoken in the wrong circumstances becomes functionally untrue. It becomes a means of denial, a form of ideology. To maintain contra a psychological determinism that the human person is possessed of freedom is undoubtedly fitting and true. And telling an individual that she is free to choose may be for that person, at a difficult moment in her life, a gesture of

---

[9] On the concept of "second nature" or "sedimented history" in its bearing upon psychology, see Russell Jacoby, *Social Amnesia: A Critique of Conformist Psychology from Adler to Laing* (Boston: Beacon Press, 1975), pp. 4, 31, 65. Despite its polemical character, or perhaps because of it, Jacoby's book is a rich source of critical insight. On the concept more generally, see Adorno, *Negative Dialectics*, p. 163, and the discussion of reification in Gillian Rose, *The Melancholy Science: An Introduction to the Thought of Theodor W. Adorno* (New York: Columbia University Press, 1978), pp. 43–51. See also Metz, *Faith in History and Society*, p. 105.

choose may be for that person, at a difficult moment in her life, a gesture of trust and assurance. But the very same words spoken at another moment may evince a bland insensitivity to what the person is, at that moment, going through. And spoken in the abstract, it may come as an empty truth which mocks the reality—much as the formally accurate statement that all persons in a certain society enjoy equal rights may gloss over the fact that some happen to exercise those rights from positions of economic privilege while others are acutely disadvantaged.

The challenges are multiple, then. And to know which is real at which moment requires the unceasing exercise of a concrete and compassionate discernment.

3. The real reductionism

How then are we to discern the present challenge to theology? I shall offer just a few remarks in closing. The common critique has rightly perceived that more is at stake in Freud than the fate of a particular theory. Psychoanalysis is a movement and an institution; it impacts upon our culture. And insofar as it propounds a diminished image of the self, it contributes to the creation of a one-dimensional society.

Now regarding contemporary culture, Victor Preller has made an astute observation. "In the modern world," he writes, ". . . a basic source of anxiety is the underlying suspicion and fear that the mind of man has in fact exhausted the nature of the real. To prove that it does not—to hold out the logical possibility of a God who might care—is tantamount to psychological salvation."[10] The remark takes reductionism seriously, to the point of recognizing that our very sense of reality has been affected. Further, it helps one understand why the popular psychological movements should have struck such a responsive chord despite their lack of critical depth. Because of the underlying anxiety that the one-dimensional world of a controlling technology may in fact be all there is, the most meager suggestion to the contrary, even a mysticism of jogging, may be *felt as* a subjective, experiential liberation. As Hegel declares in a similar context, "by the little which now satisfies the Spirit, we can measure the extent of its loss."[11]

Clearly there is a danger here. In a situation where there is such urgent need for any glimmering of transcendence, the theological task gets short-circuited. Theology becomes the errand boy of affirmation. It must be said, therefore, that precisely *because* the ravages of reductionism are so all-pervasive, the threat cannot be met head on. We cannot simply settle—as we are pressed by the urgency of the task to settle—for carving out a little

[10] Victor Preller, *Divine Science and the Science of God* (Princeton: Princeton University Press, 1967), p. 31.

[11] G. W. F. Hegel, *Phenomenology of Spirit*, trans. A. V. Miller (Oxford: Clarendon Press, 1977), p. 5.

space for subjectivity, a little space for freedom and transcendence. For it is just such compartmentalization of the realm of freedom to one side, the realm of determinism to the other—the language of poetry to one side, the language of fact to the other—which creates the one-dimensional world.[12]

The phenomenon of human diminishment is all too real and we ourselves, in our very forms of thought, are not exempt. For that very reason the matter cannot be addressed by ad hoc measures or alliances of convenience. Indeed, in the end it must be addressed by nothing less than the entirety of the Christian story, from creation through redemption. The challenge of psychology to theology is finally the challenge for theology to be itself—in all its positive fullness, in all its critical power.

[12] Cf. Max Horkheimer, "The End of Reason" in *The Essential Frankfurt School Reader*, ed. Andrew Arato and Eike Gebhardt (New York: Urizen Books, 1978); Jacques Ellul, *Hope in Time of Abandonment*, trans. C. Edward Hopkin (New York: Seabury Press, 1973).

CHAPTER ONE
BEYOND HUMANISTIC PSYCHOLOGY

> *A society is renewed when its*
> *humblest element acquires a value.*
> Ignazio Silone

Three books, Paul Ricoeur's *Freud and Philosophy,* Peter Homans's *Theology After Freud,* and Don Browning's *Generative Man,* have set the terms for much of the recent discussion of the bearing of Freud upon the concerns of theology.[1] Central concepts from these works—Ricoeur's discernment of a Freudian "teleology," Homans's espousal of an "iconic" reading of Freud, Browning's delineation of Erik Erikson's notion of "generativity"—have passed into the common parlance of the field. But such recognition brings with it the risk of misappropriation. For insofar as they are thought of in terms of the positions they advocate, these books are apt to be registered simply as so many fresh and interesting perspectives on psychoanalysis. And acknowledgment, when it takes this form, may actually exacerbate the problem our writers intended to confront—namely the multiplication of perspectives in psychoanalysis, the conflict of interpretations.

As evidence of intent one need only consider the subtitles. Ricoeur calls his work *An Essay on Interpretation;* indeed in the full French title, *De l'interprétation: Essai sur Freud,* hermeneutics takes precedence. Similarly Homans presents *An Interpretive Inquiry* and Browning speaks of *Psychoanalytic Perspectives.* This nest of concerns—the strengths and limitations of pluralism, the pivotal role of interpretation—marks the writings as peculiarly contemporary works. But if the key to their contemporaneity is their engagement with certain second-order issues of hermeneutics, it is not enough to think of the writings primarily in terms of their particular points of advocacy. Thus I wish to propose a rereading with an eye to their concern for pluralism and interpretation, as a way of learning from them something of what the ongoing agenda in this interdisciplinary area needs to be.

Seen in this light, Ricoeur, Homans, and Browning demonstrate remarkable convergence, despite their considerable diversity; and the point of the convergence, I intend to argue, is a sustained critique of certain

---

[1] Paul Ricoeur, *Freud and Philosophy: An Essay on Interpretation,* trans. Denis Savage (New Haven: Yale University Press, 1970); Peter Homans, *Theology after Freud: An Interpretive Inquiry* (Indianapolis: Bobbs-Merrill, 1970); Don S. Browning, *Generative Man—Psychoanalytic Perspectives* (Philadelphia: Westminster, 1973).

assumptions which have been widespread in the area of theology and psychology. To set forth this critique will indeed require some arguing, for our
writers have deployed it unobtrusively and its full force is apparent only
when the three works are viewed synoptically. By way of anticipation we
may recall that in the 1950s there came to prominence a number of figures
who advocated, as corrective to the behaviorism and the traditional psychoanalysis then dominant, a "third-force" or "humanistic" psychology. Gordon
Allport, Abraham Maslow, Rollo May, and Carl Rogers are representative
of this loosely associated group. The openness of these psychologists to
religious concerns was warmly reciprocated from the side of theology; as
Homans observes, "the psychological writings of the third force have been
extremely attractive to pastoral and systematic theologians."[2] It is this long-
standing alliance between theology and humanistic psychology which the
writers under review have succeeded in relativizing through their sensitivity to issues of pluralism and interpretation. For this reason their work
represents a landshift in the theological assessment of Freud.

I

Typologies are a natural way of coping with the variety of perspectives
on Freud, and each of the writers makes important use of the device. Thus
much of Ricoeur's analysis posits a broad distinction between "language of
force" and "language of meaning"; and his conclusion turns on a faceoff
between an "archaeological" hermeneutic and a "teleological" hermeneutic.[3]
Homans, for his part, proposes a tripartite discrimination between a mechanistic, a dynamic, and an iconic reading of Freud; and influenced in part by
Ricoeur, his conclusion, like Ricoeur's, sets forth two directions of thought
or imagination: the directions of nostalgia and of hope.[4] Finally Don
Browning comes forward as if to complete the progression from Ricoeur's
two-part distinction through Homan's threefold discrimination by offering
four theories of human good. These are the accomodational, the regressive,
the progressive and the dialectically progressive responses.[5]

Now how are these typologies used? Here it seems to me that a passage
from Ricoeur is emblematic of a collective shift in thought about Freud.
The key to the passage is its dogged insistence, across various modalities,
upon a crucial balance or dialectic between two perspectives within psychoanalysis. Ricoeur addresses the more troublesome of these perspectives,
namely, that which relies heavily upon such mechanistic terms as "energy,"
"drive," and "repression"—what he has called the "language of force." The

[2] Homans, *Theology after Freud*, p. 188.
[3] Ricoeur, *Freud and Philosophy*, pp. 65–67, 92.
[4] Homans, *Theology after Freud*, pp. 14, 204ff.
[5] Browning, *Generative Man*, pp. 11–31.

temptation is to junk such talk altogether. But for a philosophic critique of Freud, Ricoeur contends,

> the essential point concerns what I call the place of that energy discourse. Its place, it seems to me, lies at the intersection of desire and language; we will attempt to account for this place by the idea of an archeology of the subject. The intersection of the "natural" and the "signifying" is the point where the instinctual drives are "represented" by affects and ideas; consequently the coordination of the economic language and the intentional language is the main question of this epistemology and cannot be avoided by reducing either language to the other.[6]

To the one side Ricoeur ranges "desire," "the natural," "economic language," and "force language"—to the other side, "language" generally, "the signifying," specifically "intentional language" and "meaning language." And he holds that the heart of psychoanalysis is a peculiar activity, some "archaeology of the subject," which can occur only at the intersection of these two disparate strands. Ricouer insists that "this mixed discourse is the raison d'être of psychoanalysis."[7]

Oddities of language aside, Ricoeur's programmatic statement may serve as the key to a common stance among our three writers. I would propose that all might subscribe to the following theses. (1) While an exclusively mechanistic reading of Freud is inadequate to the fullness of his thought, a mechanistic *aspect* must be recognized. (2) The mechanistic aspect is not arbitrary; it may be associated more or less closely with a regressive *direction* of psychic processes. (3) The regressive movement (and perhaps the mechanistic vocabulary as well, depending on how closely it be associated with the movement) is not to be rejected flatly in favor of an alternative thrust; the regressive movement may be deemed to have positive significance *in its own right*. (4) Therefore an appropriate theory of human good, while it will not be a solely "regressive" response, will not be one-dimensionally "progressive" either. It may be characterized as *"dialectically progressive."*[8]

The distinctiveness of this collective stance toward Freud sharpens as one comes to appreciate its tacit polemic. To place it so, we may fashion a modest typology of our own. Let us look more closely at what is involved in the distinction we have just made, borrowing from Browning, between a "progressive" and a "dialectically progressive" reading of Freud. What is meant by a (merely) "progressive" view? Our response must be doubly hedged. First, we are trafficking in types; it is a separate question how they apply to cases *x*, *y*, and *z*. Secondly, since our governing interest is in

---

[6] Ricoeur, *Freud and Philosophy*, p. 395.
[7] Ibid., p. 65.
[8] Cf. Browning, *Generative Man*, p. 30.

Ricoeur, Homans, and Browning, we will be portraying the types as they understand them, rather than assuming an independent point of view. But all cautions duly posted, it remains that typologies, even when polemical, may have a diagnostic usefulness. And to those who are at all conversant with the folkways which prevail in the borderland of religion and psychology, the progressivist concerns will have a familiar ring.[9]

The progressivist type is crucially shaped by its determination to take a stand against Freudian reductionism. Positively it speaks on behalf of certain values which reductionism would reject. The progressive may yield to the reductionist the title of "Freudian," preferring a broader "humanistic" base. Or the progressive may argue that the reductionist has done violence to Freud himself; in this case the very title of "Freudian" will be in dispute. But whatever the tactical variations, the progressivist argument will characteristically touch upon three familiar steps. (1) A distinction is drawn between sides or *aspects* of the self. Yes, the argument runs, Freud has pointed up aspects of the psyche which may perhaps be portrayed, more or less accurately, by mechanistic metaphors. But surely we must never forget that the psyche shows another, more human face as well. Here the self transcends such mechanistic imagery; one must rather adopt such terms as "personhood," "meaning," "community," and "creativity." (2) The aspects so distinguished may be depicted hierarchically; one may speak of higher and lower *levels*. At the same time, speaking of "higher" and "lower" may serve to introduce the value questions which reductionism has conspired to neglect. (3) Finally there may be added to the image of hierarchy a temporal dimension. As Homans has remarked, the distinguishing of *stages* is a hallmark of the progressivist type.[10] And as with the hierarchy, so too the genesis may be cast in descriptive or prescriptive terms, or most likely in some combination of the two. Indeed the teleological convergence of descriptive and prescriptive viewpoints is often and not unnaturally received as a sort of ontological endorsement of the progressivist intent.

The progressivist type is disarming in its appeal. Unlike the mechanistic approach, which bids fair to reduce psychology to the hydraulics of psychic plumbing, the progressive is anchored in common sense. Further, the position has power to stir the fires of human aspiration. And thanks to this convergence of acceptance and aspiration, it is well placed to furnish

---

[9] Browning's key instance of the progressivist type is Erich Fromm, though Browning finds Fromm capable of transcending the type (Browning, p. 135). Homans's criticism refers "primarily to the work of Allport, Maslow, and Carl Rogers, although by implication it includes such earlier neo-Freudians as Sullivan, Horney and Fromm and, in ego psychology, the work of Erikson as well" (Homans, *Theology after Freud*, p. 186). That Browning and Homans should differ in their placing of Erikson is fair warning against viewing our three authors in monolithic fashion. At the same time, disagreement as to the application of a type need not preclude substantial accord regarding the type's nature and limitations.

[10] Homans, *Theology after Freud*, p. 187.

sorely needed counsel in coping with the day-to-day. We are offered illumination on the art of loving, guidance toward self-fulfillment. And there is still more: for along with its edifying practicality the position boasts in the image of hierarchy a conceptual framework which provides, at least potentially, a hermeneutic of great sophistication.

It may be rash to resist a psychology of such power. Certainly it must seem ungracious to dissent from an appeal which is so earnestly humanistic. One need hardly wonder that many theologians should have felt that, whatever else might be unresolved in the field of psychology, they at least knew who their friends were. Thus it comes as an anomaly to find each of our three authors distancing himself from the progressivist, "humanistic" view. And if upon inspection it should emerge that the reasons for this divergence are not idiosyncratic but systematic and deep, we may have something more than an anomaly. We may have a fundamental shift in the parameters of the ongoing discussion of Freud.[11]

II

The manner of Peter Homans's dissent is, in effect, to question whether the image of hierarchy really does function as an integrative framework after all. In his view the humanistic psychologies amount to "a moral psychology of socialization."[12] At best their exhortations reflect a confusing of ends and means, as if the telos of transcending socialization could be attained simply by consciously attending to transcendence or as if the higher were to be achieved by resolutely turning one's back upon the lower. "These theories of personality claim that transcendence can be negotiated theoretically and can be achieved developmentally without reference to the dynamics of repression. . . ."[13] This is to charge that in practice the image of hierarchy functions not for integrative interpretation but for *selective orientation*. We are not so much presented with a whole as pointed toward the "higher." And that brings a division between "higher" and "lower" which is no less disabling for its being unintended. In effect a premature conflation of descriptive and normative viewpoints has masked a recurrence of the classic split between subject and object. Worse, it has contributed to that split.[14] Nor is the problem simply one of flawed execution; it roots back to

---

[11] That the criticizing of humanistic psychology is not simply a Freudian preoccupation becomes apparent when one turns to the much-discussed work of James Hillman, whose background is primarily Jungian. His "Critique of Modern Humanism's Psychology," in *Re-Visioning Psychology* (New York: Harper and Row, 1975), pp. 180-89, is indeed a more explicit attack than any of the treatments presently under discussion.

[12] Homans, *Theology after Freud*, p. 186.

[13] Ibid., p. 187.

[14] Ibid., p. 188.

the very first of progressivism's logical steps, to its manner of distinguishing aspects:

> Such personality theories as Allport's, Fromm's, Rogers's, and
> Sullivan's, like theological existentialism, in their own way make a
> fatal distinction between the developmental and whatever lies beyond
> mere socialization. In so doing, they lack the necessary presup-
> positional equipment for a generic intersubjectivity, which would
> undergird such distinctions as these between earlier and later, regres-
> sion and development, and childhood and selfhood.[15]

The allusion to theological existentialism is for Homans a telling indictment. The burden of his book is that the tradition variously represented by
Reinhold Niebuhr and Paul Tillich has failed to supply us with a vision
which could hold steadily in view the theological and the psychological. It
has offered us rather "a theology of the gaps"—countenancing, even cele-
brating, disjunction and discontinuity.[16] Thus Homans's critique of progressivism comports with the fundamental argument of his book. We may
conclude, therefore, that although his explicit treatments of the type are
brief and episodic, his distrust of it is fundamental.

Homans's position so interpreted may be translated and amplified in the
vocabulary of Paul Ricoeur. What Homans calls a failure to "undergird"
and thus integrate certain distinctions is, in Ricoeur's terms, a surrendering
of the vital "archeology," a sundering of "economic language" and "intentional language." Who fails at this critical juncture will tend ineluctably to
absorb one language into the other. Just as surely as the reductionist isolated
economic language, the progressivist elevates the intentional. Their distortions are mirror images of one another—and the progressivist is not the less
misguided of the two. For as the title of an important section of *Freud and
Philosophy* admonishes, "Psychoanalysis is Not Phenomenology."[17]

The contrast between phenomenology and psychoanalysis, indeed the
"conflict" between them, is central to Ricoeur's hermeneutic.[18] A point of
entrée into this conflict is Ricoeur's remark that a peculiar fusion of "the

---

[15] Ibid. Emphasis added.

[16] Ibid., pp. 52ff., 88ff.

[17] Ricoeur, *Freud and Philosophy*, p. 390.

[18] Paul Ricoeur, *The Conflict of Interpretations: Essays in Hermeneutics* (Evanston: Northwestern University Press, 1974), pp. 99ff. Some explicit historical ties can be traced between progress-
ivist psychology and the philosophic tradition of phenomenology. See Herbert Spiegelberg, *Phenomenology in Psychology and Psychiatry: A Historical Introduction* (Evanston: Northwestern University Press, 1972), e.g. pp. 148–57. But for the connection I wish to suggest, historical influence is less important than a certain broad conceptual affinity. It is the sort of link touched upon by Browning when he muses, "we wonder if finally all is reduced to consciousness and lucidity in productive man" (Browning, *Generative Man*. p. 138).

infra- and the supralinguistic is perhaps the most notable language achievement of the Freudian unconscious."[19] It will be in keeping with Ricoeur's
argument if we extrapolate his formula to say that *the fusion of the intersubjective and the infra-personal* may be the most notable practical achievement of
Freudian psychoanalysis. For "one cannot overestimate the amazing audacity
of this discovery, namely of treating the intersubjective relationship as
technique."[20] Indeed it might almost be said that the innovation of psychoanalysis is to have made of the I-Thou relationship the object, and even the
means, of *manipulation.* Nothing could be more contrary to the phenomenologist's first dictum of disengagement, of "bracketing" the phenomena, than
such programmatic intervention. Like Homans's progressivist, the phenomenologist would prefer to negotiate transcendence "without reference to the
dynamics of repression." But for the Freudian analyst such technique is
indispensable; and Ricoeur as I understand him argues that this indispens-
ability of technique is reflected in the irreducibility of Freud's "language of
force," his mechanistic metaphors. Ricoeur says of this language that it
portrays the person insofar as he or she "has been and remains a Thing."[21]
Functionally this is to say that the force language portrays persons insofar as
their intersubjective processes must properly be *treated as* things. For the
analytic technique is centered upon "resistance, transference, repetition. . . ."
This vocabulary and this sequence constitute "the core of the analytic
situation."[22] Frustration, for example, is not simply examined as a problem;
it is adopted as a tool:

> If the patient's suffering becomes mitigated, "we must reinstate it
> elsewhere in the form of some appreciable privation." Thus the
> analyst's work . . . is . . . a struggle against substitute satisfactions—
> precisely in the transference where the patient is looking for such
> satisfaction. For the phenomenologist, this technique of frustration
> is the most surprising aspect of the analytic method; he can no
> doubt understand the rule of veracity, but not the principle of frus-
> tration: the latter can only be practiced.[23]

Thus the thread joining beginning and end of Ricoeur's discussion is the
discovery that "the irreducibility of the energy aspect" is a transcription of
the fact that "psychoanalysis is a unique and irreducible form of praxis."[24]

---

[19] Ricoeur, *Freud and Philosophy*, p. 405.

[20] Ibid., p. 406.

[21] Ibid., p. 114. Emphasis altered.

[22] Ibid., p. 415.

[23] Ibid., p. 417. Sigmund Freud, "Lines of Advance in Psycho-Analytic Therapy," in *The
Standard Edition of the Complete Psychological Works of Sigmund Freud,* trans. under general editorship of James Strachey, 24 vols. (London: Hogarth Press, 1924), 17:163.

[24] Ibid., pp. 404, 418.

III

But Ricoeur's argument, like Homans's, must be seen in context if its full force is to be felt. Here the original title, *De l'interprétation,* is significant. Ricoeur's earlier study in the interpretation of myth, *The Symbolism of Evil,* traced the manner in which an early participation in symbol is jolted and transformed by the "Copernican revolution" of an emerging self-awareness.[25] Proud of its newly-discovered prerogatives, proud to have found that it is immeasurably more than a mere object among objects, consciousness withdraws from its initial credulity, becomes alienated and is drawn to a demythologized reading of its earlier beliefs. But pride is a double-edged term which may readily pass from robust self-affirmation to insensitivity and self-inflation. "The self becomes detached and exiles itself into what the Stoics have already called the circularity of the soul . . . the circle which I form with myself."[26]

Now in Ricoeur's eyes, the phenomenology of Edmund Husserl amounts to an effort to fashion from just such self-awareness a normative philosophic program. The effort represents an inestimable achievement, "a conquest of criticism over naturalistic (or mundane) naiveté."[27] But the proposal is crippled by a certain "second-level naiveté" which its very achievement serves to mask. This is "a transcendental naiveté which takes the place of the naturalistic one. The transcendental reflection creates the illusion that philosophy could be a reflection without a spiritual discipline (*ascèse*), without a purification of its own seeing."[28] Here is dogmatic slumber of another sort, which must needs be shaken by "a second Copernican revolution." And the prophet of that revolution is none other than Sigmund Freud. In the words of Don Ihde's illuminating commentary:

> The threat . . . is the issue of false consciousness which throughout Ricoeur's philosophy has been equated with the possibility of a transcendental illusion, the "circle the self makes with itself." Phenomenology must be limited to prevent this circle and Freud becomes the figure who symptomatically serves this function.[29]

Ricoeur's brief section on phenomenology emerges as the linchpin of an argument which has been abuilding throughout his philosophy. And indeed

---

[25] Paul Ricoeur, *The Symbolism of Evil,* trans. Emerson Buchanan (New York: Harper and Row, 1967), pp. 347ff.

[26] Paul Ricoeur, *Freedom and Nature: The Voluntary and the Involuntary,* trans. Erazim V. Kohak (Evanston: Northwestern University Press, 1966), p. 14.

[27] Paul Ricoeur, *Husserl: An Analysis of his Phenomenology,* trans. Edward G. Ballard and Lester E. Embree (Evanston: Northwestern University Press, 1967), p. 228.

[28] Ibid., p. 232.

[29] Don Ihde, *Hermeneutic Phenomenology: The Philosophy of Paul Ricoeur* (Evanston: Northwestern University Press, 1971), p. 140. In this treatment of reflection and naiveté in Ricoeur, I am following closely Ihde's very helpful exposition (pp. 14–20, 140ff.).

nothing short of this crucial "symptomatic" significance of Freud could explain why the long labor of writing *Freud and Philosophy* was permitted to interrupt the progression of Ricoeur's multi-volume *Philosophy of the Will*. For Ricoeur as for Homans the critique of progressivist psychology is integral to a larger and fundamental task.

Thus has Freud the oft-maligned reductionist become, in breaking the closed circle of phenomenology, the agent of greater openness! Our theme of the pluralism of psychological perspectives adds piquancy to the ironies which abound at this juncture in Ricoeur's philosophy. For not only is Freud the agent of openness—the instrument of that openness is to be his "language of force," the most hermetic aspect of his thought! Earlier we suggested that psychoanalysis represents a fusion of the intersubjective and the infrapersonal, that it exceeds phenomenology at each limit and that it exceeds it the more in fusing the extremes. We can now see more clearly how that proposal pays off by exploding the cloture of phenomenology. Ihde notes that "phenomenology remains a thematization of consciousness and thus is blind to any distortion which may occur at the very origin of meaning."[30] The task of psychoanalysis is to address just such infrapersonal distortions. But it does so in awareness that distortions are generated by certain intersubjective contexts. Thus Ricoeur can say of the force language (though he says it after considerable interpretation), "The intersubjective constitution of desire is the profound truth of the Freudian theory of the libido."[31]

So fused in its diagnosis, psychoanalysis is even more disconcerting in its remedy. Here we return to the instructive matter of technique. To cure, the process of transference is indispensable—the remedy is modeled upon, if not restricted to, the analytic session. Transference is the needle's eye and the impossibility of circumventing it is doubly wounding to the pride of reflective consciousness. Consciousness is shaken from its dreams of self-sufficiency by this reminder of intersubjectivity, most pointedly by the necessary reliance upon another self. And consciousness' firm sense that self-awareness has elevated it above being a mere object among objects is humbled by the treatment of "the intersubjective relationship as technique." Quite nearly, consciousness is treated as a thing. Thus the circle of the conscious, personal self is pried open by just that aspect of Freud's theory which portrays the person insofar as he or she "has been and remains a Thing."

If Freud's force language functions to provide this check upon the pretensions of the more phenomenological meaning language, his retention of a "mixed discourse" may not be quite the muddle it is often taken to be. It is a commonplace of progressivist criticism to hold that Freud was a genius in his age but a child of his time, gifted with certain insights but disastrously enamoured of a mechanistic physics. As Freud himself drily

---

[30] Ibid., p. 151.
[31] Ricoeur, *Freud and Philosophy*, p. 387.

remarked, "First they call me a genius and then they proceed to reject all my views."[32] Our argument suggests that in some part Freud may have designed his mixed discourse to be a standing reminder, an arena in which two necessary perspectives could abut and relativize one another. If so, there is irony in the reflection that the humanistic psychologies, for all their undoubted earnestness about being personally open, are, when considered systematically, the less open to a plurality of views and to the possibility of "non-humanistic" interpretation.

IV

We close our survey by considering somewhat more briefly Browning's *Generative Man*. The book might well be discussed at length, for its analysis of Erich Fromm as a case study of the progressivist view lends specificity to points which Ricoeur and Homans make in a more general way. But by the same token the explicitness of Browning's criticism and its clear placement within a comprehensive typology renders commentary less essential.

Let us begin by recalling that it is Browning who gave us the term "progressive." He more than Homans is drawn to the type for its robust and rightminded celebration of the active, productive life; within it he finds room for many of the points he would wish to make.[33] And yet the spaciousness is never quite enough. Here it is useful to quote Browning in full, for his treatment suggests the subtlety which is needed if one is to rightly locate the point of one's divergence from the humanistic view.

> As we have already seen, in his portrait of productive man's relation to himself, there are certain ways in which Fromm does take account of that which is ontogenetically and phylogenetically early. We have seen that productiveness as a progressive advance includes within it man's primitive desire for union. Productiveness also includes, as we have noted, the so-called nonproductive orientations; when the passive nonproductive orientations are organized and guided by the productive orientations, they take on a new and positive meaning. Finally, we have seen that productiveness recapitulates at historical and existential levels of existence the fundamental urge to produce new life.
>
> What, then, has Fromm left out? Why do we still suspect that Fromm has a bias toward the high and progressive? Why do we continue to distrust his efforts to incorporate the archaic into productivity? Our suspicions indeed have reasons. It is one thing to say that the phylogenetically and ontogenetically low has value when stated in the context of productivity. This Fromm often does. *It is*

[32] Joseph Wortis, *Fragments of an Analysis with Freud* (New York: Simon and Schuster, 1954), p. 142.
[33] Browning, *Generative Man*, p. 135.

something else, however, to state that meaning of the ontogenetically and phylogenetically low in terms of their meaning for themselves. This Fromm does not do at all.[34]

Fromm says the right things, in effect, but says them in a context which undercuts their truth. What is required, as Browning states emphatically, is a context which could prove sufficiently *dialectical.*[35] For it is vital that the earlier and lower aspects be accorded a certain conceptual independence, that they be recognized as having meaning in their own right—"meaning for themselves."

Now in the strictest sense, of course, nothing has meaning simply for itself; and similarly, independence is always relative. The proper function of saying that *a* has a certain independence is generally to affirm that the lines of dependency do not all run in one direction: in some ways *b* depends upon *a*. Thus in the present case one would want to show that the later and higher are in certain respects dependent upon the lower and earlier. But therein lies the rub. For once we have shown that much, what is to prevent us from a relapse into thinking of the lower simply in terms of the service it provides the higher—and from undercutting thereby the very independence we had intended to assert?[36]

In this light we can understand how it is that the progressivist type can say the right things and yet manage to come out wrong. Indeed we can see how the type comes out wrong by virtue of saying the right things, simply by saying them undialectically. Browning's study of Fromm issues in a conclusion which might have seemed a contradiction in terms, namely, that *holism is not enough.* The "whole" is specious if undialectical; and among the essentials of a dialectical relationship, two are of special note. (1) There must be a stringent critique of the "higher" aspects or perspectives. (2) There must be a clear and rigorous distinction between the "higher," on the one hand, and the comprehensive framework, which would encompass both high and low, on the other. Obviously these points reinforce one another: to subject the "higher" to a larger framework is already an implicit critique. And both points share a single aim, that of halting at the outset the subtle chemistry which begins with the higher as the ultimate value and ends with it as the sole reality. Once again we are returned to our theme of the pluralism of psychological perspectives. For a dismaying pattern connects Browning's remark that "nowhere does Fromm explicitly pay attention to children" and

---

[34] Ibid., pp. 135–36.

[35] Ibid., pp. 21, 135.

[36] Bertell Ollman argues that a concept of "internal relations," drawn from Hegel but previously formulated by Spinoza and Leibniz, plays a decisive role in the critical thought of Marx. One wonders whether a similar notion might not be implicitly at work in the best of psychoanalytic reflection. See Bertell Ollman, *Alienation: Marx's Conception of Man in Capitalist Society* (Cambridge: Cambridge University Press, 1971), pp. 26–40, *passim.*

his subsequent worry: "we wonder if finally all is reduced to consciousness and lucidity in productive man."[37] Once again one feels the insistent, centripetal drift toward the circle which consciousness makes with itself.

V

Our survey has sought to bring forward the larger concerns, and thereby the express or implicit norms, which underlie three recent critiques of humanistic psychology. Perhaps it may be taken as a tribute to the cogency of that cumulative critique and to the urgency of its concerns if we now attempt to raise the same questions regarding the positive positions which the critics themselves have severally advanced. This is one way of asking what our own agenda ought to be. But if within the bounds of the present essay we are to apply criticisms as subtle as those we have sketched to books as complex as those we have drawn from, some tactical compromise must be made. I propose therefore to confine my discussion to Ricoeur and to simply allow the criticism made of him to stand as open questions regarding the work of Homans and Browning.[38]

Progressivism was deeply shaped by its overriding concern to respond to the challenge of reductionism. The type showed no comparable concern to resist the collapse of psychoanalysis into phenomenology, and at times it expressly moves toward such an identification. Ricoeur has been immensely illuminating as to why this tendency should be resisted; yet it may be argued that his actual reading of Freud reflects a distinct though inadvertent bias in the progressivist sense. As a convenient case we may examine in some detail his treatment of the earliest and purest example of Freud's "force language," the "Project for a Scientific Psychology."

Written in 1895, the "Project" remained unpublished until 1950. It represents a remarkable speculative attempt to sketch a psychology in terms continuous with the language of neurology. In the words of his programmatic statement: "The project involves two principal ideas: (1) That what distinguishes activity from rest is to be regarded as a quantity (Q) subject to the general laws of motion. (2) That it is to be assumed that the material particles in question are the neuron."[39] Surely this passage must stand as a *locus classicus* of Freud's "language of force." Yet Ricoeur succeeds in showing even in this extreme case that certain concessions to the givens of human experience were inescapable and that even this minimal concern was

---

[37] Browning, *Generative Man*, pp. 136, 138.

[38] I consider Ricoeur's Freud study in greater detail elsewhere. See Walter Lowe, *Mystery and the Unconscious: A Study in the Thought of Paul Ricoeur* (Metuchen, N.J.: Scarecrow Press, 1977). The present analysis is adapted from portions of that work, pp. 99–102, 114–16.

[39] Sigmund Freud, *The Origins of Psycho-Analysis: Letters to Wilhelm Fliess, Drafts and Notes: 1887-1902*, ed. Marie Bonaparte, Anna Freud, and Ernst Kris, trans. Eric Mosbacher and James Strachey (New York: Basic Books, 1954), p. 355.

enough to drive Freud's "Project" into incoherence. As an example, for the general laws of motion to be applicable, one must posit a closed energy system. But the crucial notion of satisfaction prohibits one from viewing the psyche as such a system because the notion implicates "the external world (food, sexual partner)."[40] Or as a further example, the laws of motion assume that one begins with a free flow of energy. But within the psyche some energy is ineluctably "bound."[41] It was the mounting pressure of considerations such as these that led to the project's abandonment.

Ricoeur's assessment of this chapter in the prehistory of psychoanalysis is to discern in Freud's grudging admission of what he was later to call secondary processes the first stirrings of an authentically "hermeneutical" psychology. Vestiges of the quasi-mechanistic viewpoint were never to be entirely erased, Freud remained determinist to the end; but already in this most recalcitrant of his writings there lies the germ of a perspective which will not be covertly anatomical, but genuinely "psychic."[42] Now all this is true enough. But it must be remarked that Ricoeur's exposition with its stress upon Freud's move away from a flat reductionism has been such as to invite a progressivist reading of the Freudian evolution. Yet Ricoeur's conclusion posts no warnings against such an undialectical interpretation. Rather, in its overriding concern to rebut the reductionist view, it has allied itself with the progressivist stance.

The imbalance of this formative section of Ricoeur's exposition becomes clearer as one gains sight of a quite different side of the Freudian evolution. This alternative reading may be approached indirectly, by a further spelling-out of the progressivist view. The progressivist might reason as follows. Freud began by postulating a psychic machine which was in principle autonomous, "a machine which in a moment would run of itself."[43] But in acknowledging certain secondary processes, Freud surrendered some part of the machine's autonomy. The machine proved dependent upon certain external relations; and even within the psyche it required certain impediments to the free flow of energy. Since the machine is the forerunner of the Freudian id, the progressivist reckons in anticipation that Freud has already placed constraints upon the autonomy of the id; and thus by extension he has placed constraints upon the autonomy of the unconscious.

However, a little knowledge is proverbially a dangerous thing and there is no reason to suppose that a little secondary process is, per se, any better. In criticism of the progressivist reading it must be said that if Freud has acknowledged in the unconscious certain secondary processes, it is equally true that the processes have been located *in the unconscious*. One has in the

---

[40] Ricoeur, *Freud and Philosophy*, p. 77.
[41] Ibid., p. 70.
[42] Ibid., p. 83.
[43] Freud, *Origins of Psycho-Analysis*, p. 129.

nature of the processes no guarantee of the ends which they will pursue once they have slipped from conscious surveillance. To have assumed such a guarantee is the sort of rationalist fallacy to which the progressivist is prone. Recalling the two criteria which emanated from the discussion of Fromm, we may say that what is wanting at this point in Ricoeur is any sort of sustained critique of the "higher" element, the secondary processes.

VI

The needed critique becomes accessible as one attends to the obscured aspect of Freud's evolution. At the outset Freud postulated, in a pure instance of force language, "a machine which in a moment would run of itself." It is the direct consequence of the advent of secondary processes, which is to say of "bound energy," that now the machine can somewhat inhibit its immediate response. Thereby it steps back, as it were, and poses itself against its surroundings. As Ricoeur himself says of the concept of secondary process, "the scientist's disinterestedness, his ability to concentrate steadily on an idea, is thus translated into energy terms."[44] Add perception, as Freud does—and the mechanistic metaphor is transformed, the machine has become effectively *cybernetic*. This I take to be the unremarked import of Ricoeur's summary observation that "it is a point that will never change: the constant cathexis of the ego, the function of inhibiting, and reality-testing will always go together."[45] The consequence of reality-testing is that autonomy has been *limited*; that is the abiding truth of the progressivist view. But by the same stroke, by virtue of inhibition, the autonomy has been *heightened*.

If the original conception of the machine was the forerunner of the id, the revised conception is the forerunner of the *interaction* of the ego and the id. From that interaction there emerges what I have called a "higher" form of autonomy, a phrase which I hope to clarify momentarily. Now if the machine is still the same machine in any sense at all, the autonomy will in some part be placed at the service of the machine's original purposes, the purposes of the id. Thus one result of the advent of secondary processes is simply a more wily pursuit of what Freud will eventually call "the pleasure principle." When matters are viewed thus, in the light of purposes or prin-ciples, it becomes a good deal less certain that Freud is in the process of abandoning the perspective epitomized in his "language of force." And it is in any case clear that to an unspecified extent the autonomy of the uncon-scious has in fact been "heightened"—not in spite of, but because of, the introduction of secondary processes. In this observation we may have found a fulcrum for the needed critique of those processes.

[44] Ricoeur, *Freud and Philosophy*, pp. 81–82.
[45] Ibid., p. 79.

The general absence of such a countervailing perspective from Ricoeur's own reading of Freud is confirmed by another section, his summary conclusion regarding Freud's first topography. Ricoeur begins by simply reintroducing the will-o'-the-wisp notion of an autonomous affect.[46] The very idea is a shade of the long-abandoned "Project," but it is the bête noir of the progressivist view. In the course of his discussion of the first topography Ricoeur has shown that the concept of pure drive or pure primary process, which concept must underlie any notion of a radically independent affect, is an abstraction or a Kantian idea.[47] To couch one's summary of the entire topography in terms of what has befallen such an abstraction is to entrap discussion at a rudimentary level. Specifically it is to confine discussion to de facto terms. As Ricoeur frames the matter, it happens that in point of fact Freud's concept of affect always did retain a certain linkage to ideas or presentations.[48] Freud's particular conclusions, his interweaving of force language and meaning language, are divested of all logical *necessity*. The balance or fusion which is "the raison d'être of psychoanalysis" seems no more than an idiosyncracy.

Therefore, in criticism of the drift of Ricoeur's remarks, we must hold emphatically that *the autonomy of affect is not the autonomy of the unconscious*. So true is this that the decline of the one may actually signal an increase of the other! An autonomous affect would move freely toward expression or discharge. But it would also move directly—which is to say that its movement would be as mechanical, and thus as predictable, as the course of an electric current. In principle the "independent" affect would have no independence of the predictions of a conscious observer. It would be "auto-nomous" in the root sense that it would follow its own law unencumbered; but its law would remain entirely public. The autonomy of the *unconscious* in contrast is predicated upon, precisely, the partial *inhibition* of the free flow of affect. Through such caution the unconscious, as an interplay of primary and secondary processes, manages to keep one step ahead of conscious observation, or at least it tries to do so. This is what is intended in saying that it attains to an autonomy which is limited but higher. It is this aspect of Freud's evolution which Ricoeur's exposition has obscured.[49]

But perhaps Ricoeur will act to right the balance further on. Turning from Ricoeur's exposition to the more systematic "Dialectic" which concludes *Freud and Philosophy*, one finds that the crucial section bears the promising rubric, "Dialectic: Archeology and Teleology."[50] The argument here turns

---

[46] Ibid., pp. 146–47.
[47] Ibid., p. 116.
[48] Ibid., pp. 150–51.
[49] Which sort of autonomy is meant, for instance, when Ricoeur reiterates that "the topography and its naturalistic naiveté are suited to the very essence of desire, inasmuch as desires are 'indestructible,' 'immortal,' that is to say, always prior to language and culture"? Ibid.
[50] Ibid., p. 459.

on a confrontation between Freud and Hegel. But Ricoeur leads us beyond a mere juxtaposition of the two figures or a vague proposal that they be viewed as mutually complementary. He undertakes to demonstrate the complementarity on grounds intrinsic to each of the two: he displays a "teleology" latent within Freud and an "archeology" which is a secondary but essential moment in Hegel. For, "whereas Hegel links an explicit teleology of mind or spirit to an implicit archeology of life and desire, Freud links a thematized archeology of the unconscious to an unthematized teleology of the process of becoming conscious."[51] To have yoked together two such disparate thinkers in a manner which does violence to neither is unquestionably an argumentative feat of a high order. The questions I wish to raise come from a position which is enormously indebted to Ricoeur's accomplishment.

Yet questions there are. To recall once again our first requirement of a dialectical formulation: has consciousness undergone the needed critique? Ricoeur's thesis that both Freud and Hegel criticize immediacy suggests that they may cooperate in certain respects—but it also may suggest that in the very last analysis Hegel may have nothing indispensable to learn from Freud. Latently at least, it is all already there. The blithe reader might suppose that Ricoeur were condoning the possibility of simply opting for Hegel, with a passing nod to Freud. The suggestion so flies in the face of Ricoeur's express intent that it might be dismissed out of hand, were it not for a further consideration. This has to do with the second of our criteria regarding the dialectical: has a clear and rigorous distinction been made between the "higher" element, on the one hand, and the comprehensive framework encompassing both high and low, on the other hand? Two passages from Ihde's commentary may suffice to locate the problem in Ricoeur. Both have to do with Ricoeur's tactic of demonstrating complementarity between the two thinkers. First, here is Ihde on the aim or intent of that tactic: "the excess of psychoanalysis must be balanced by an equal excess from within reflection—and the figure to provide this excess is Hegel."[52] And now here is Ihde on the result:

> Hegel inverts Freud, and Ricoeur ultimately sides with Hegel. . . . In the last analysis the self is constituted primarily in terms of progression: "the positing or emergence of the self is inseparable from its production through a progressive synthesis." Thus at the end of this set of dialectical exercises the weighted focus of phenomenology—now in Hegelian guise—is restored.[53]

Where in Ricoeur is there a clear and rigorous distinguishing of Hegel the

---

[51] Ibid., p. 461.
[52] Ihde, p. 155.
[53] Ibid., p. 159; Ricoeur, *Freud and Philosophy*, p. 464.

"excessive" counter-element from Hegel the adequate, embracing whole—Hegel the "antithesis," as it were, from Hegel the "synthesis"?

The distinguishing of uses of Hegel becomes the distinguishing of aspects of Hegel himself. To find that distinction pressed with the needed vigor, we must turn to another thinker whom Ricoeur occasionally invokes as guide, namely Martin Heidegger. For the sake of brevity in presenting Heidegger's reading of Hegel, I must draw upon a commentator once again; and for the sake of clarity in making the critical point, I must adduce one more long quotation. The commentator is W. B. Macomber.

> But there is ambiguity concealed in Hegel's thinking, even in the *Phenomenology.* The question is whether the context of intelligibility implied in all conscious experience is a reflection of the movement of consciousness or a timeless order which makes such movement possible, whether truth is to be seen *in* conflict or *emerging out of* conflict, whether consciousness is to be grounded in itself or to point beyond itself, and whether contradiction is ultimately to prove the limitation of understanding or rather, in being taken up into understanding, to testify to its omnipotence. As the ultimate context of intelligibility Hegel's absolute is the counterpart of Heidegger's world. The question is whether there is anything *besides* the world. In the *Phenomenology* the absolute appears in a tenuous equilibrium with incessant unrest, negativity, doubt, despair, and death. But in the later works this equilibrium is lost.[54]

My point is almost commonsensical. Only a context which guards that equilibrium can contain Freud without stifling him. Only a context sensitive to "incessant unrest, negativity, doubt, despair, and death" can hear what he has to say. To dwell on something "more" which might lie beyond such conflict is precisely that "excess" which issues not in more but in less—and which devolves thereby from being the fitting context to being a mere element within a larger, corrective equilibrium.

It is no secret that the conflictual reading of Hegel steers the *Phenomenology* in the direction of Heidegger's own thought. And in the long run Ricoeur does seem prepared to affirm Heidegger as his philosophic sponsor.[55] I would urge that for those who share Ricoeur's concern for a critique of humanistic psychology, his study of Freud will prove most serviceable when viewed in this Heideggerian context. After all, it is Heidegger who cleared the way for a critique of "humanism" in philosophy.[56]

---

[54] W. B. Macomber, *The Anatomy of Disillusion: Martin Heidegger's Notion of Truth* (Evanston: Northwestern University Press, 1967), p. 185.

[55] Ricoeur, *Conflict of Interpretations,* pp. 6–11.

[56] Martin Heidegger, "Letter on Humanism," trans. Frank A. Capuzzi and J. Glenn Gray, *Basic Writings from* Being and Time *(1927)* to The Task of Thinking *(1964),* ed. David Farrell Krell (New York: Harper and Row, 1977), pp. 189ff.

For the rest, one may find oneself reading Ricoeur "against the stream,"
contra the drift of his own thought. He has taught us why a critique of
humanistic psychology is needed, he has given us the materials with which
to proceed. But point by point that critique does not inform his actual
reading of Freud. And in consequence he himself is open to the exclusively
humanistic interpretation which he has taught us to distrust.

CHAPTER TWO
THE CASE OF PAUL RICOEUR

*Whoso means to rescue and preserve
the subjective element shall lose
it: but whoso gives it up for the
sake of the objective, shall save it.*
Karl Barth

Among contemporary writings in religious studies the work of Paul Ricoeur has attained a certain emblematic status. There seem to be few topics he has not in some fashion illumined: ranging from human freedom to narrative discourse, by way of the unconscious, the problem of evil and the parables of the New Testament. As regards method his work has been similarly far-reaching. He began with a distinctive appropriation of Husserlian phenomenology and then sought to "graft" onto phenomenology a certain use of hermeneutics. He has drawn upon structuralism and linguistic analysis, and recently he has focussed upon the hermeneutics of the written text. Throughout this intellectual pilgrimage his writings have exhibited a generosity of spirit and quick sensitivity to the currents of his times. For these reasons he has been, in the best sense of the word, a representative thinker.

But the unity of Ricoeur's work is surely more than a matter of temperament. Ricoeur himself has encouraged us to seek in his writings a certain encompassing architecture. The early study translated as *Freedom and Nature: The Voluntary and the Involuntary* presented itself as the first in a multivolume series, a *Philosophy of the Will*. Ricoeur was quite clear that by removing certain phenomenological brackets employed in *Freedom and Nature* he would proceed to *Fallible Man* and *The Symbolism of Evil*, which were indeed published in 1960, and thence to a volume of "poetics," which has yet to appear. It may be that Ricoeur's recent studies on metaphor and on narrative are to be taken as constituting the poetics, in effect. What is certain in any case is that upon completion of *The Symbolism of Evil* Ricoeur's writing veered in some unanticipated directions. *Freud and Philosophy*, a monumental study of psychoanalysis, appeared in 1965; and beyond this his thought has tended to express itself in a profusion of essays—each very rich and suggestive, but largely exploratory in character.[1]

---

[1] See Paul Ricoeur, *Freedom and Nature: The Voluntary and the Involuntary*, trans. Erazim V. Kohák (Evanston: Northwestern University Press, 1966); *The Symbolism of Evil*, trans. Emerson

How is one to assess a body of work which presents itself as being at once programmatic and open-ended? How deal with a situation in which the very richness of the writing renders the author enigmatic? These are the questions the present essay proposes to pursue. The inquiry is necessitated by the fact that once one passes beyond certain thematic generalizations about Ricoeur, and once one has acknowledged certain familiar epigrams such as "the symbol gives rise to thought," one finds that the restless, dialogic character of Ricoeur's thought—the very source of his richness—makes it increasingly difficult to locate "the Ricoeurian center." It is hard, in other words, to know where he finally comes down. And if to these perplexities one adds what I have termed the emblematic significance of Ricoeur's work—if one considers that some of us have gotten in the habit of looking to Ricoeur to help get our bearings on how things are proceeding in the field—then the question becomes more than intriguing: it becomes somewhat pressing as well. Working as we do within a field which has not been widely noted for its internal coherence, we have more than an incidental stake in asking, *is* there a Ricoeurian center? and if so, in what does it consist?

In taking up these questions, the present essay seeks to build upon the work of previous commentators, particularly Don Ihde and Patrick Bourgeois, as well as the recently published *Studies in the Philosophy of Paul Ricoeur*; thus the first section will reflect upon some proposals which have already been made regarding the question of Ricoeur's consistency.[2] Then in a second section I will venture a typology dealing with views of the relationship between the finite and the infinite, and I will test that typology as a way of accounting for the peculiar course of Ricoeur's development. A concluding section will highlight certain issues which the inquiry will have raised.

I

We may identify three lines of response regarding the question of Ricoeur's consistency. It is possible to say that in the last analysis the philosophy remains a *phenomenology*, or one can argue that the key is rather the mounting emphasis placed upon *hermeneutics*—or one can seek the answer in

---

Buchanan (New York: Harper and Row, 1967); *Fallible Man*, trans. Charles Kelbley (Chicago: Henry Regnery, 1965); *The Conflict of Interpretations: Essays in Hermeneutics*, ed. Don Ihde (Evanston: Northwestern University Press, 1974); and *Freud and Philosophy: An Essay on Interpretation*, trans. Denis Savage (New Haven: Yale University Press, 1970). Ricoeur's recent books, *Interpretation Theory: Discourse and the Surplus of Meaning* (Fort Worth: Texas Christian University Press, 1976) and *The Rule of Metaphor*, trans. Robert Czerny et al. (Toronto: University of Toronto Press, 1977) are presented as volumes of "essays" or "studies."

[2] See Don Ihde, *Hermeneutic Phenomenology: The Philosophy of Paul Ricoeur* (Evanston: Northwestern University Press, 1971); Patrick L. Bourgeois, *Extension of Ricoeur's Hermeneutic* (The Hague: Martinus Nijhoff, 1975); and *Studies in the Philosophy of Paul Ricoeur*, ed. Charles E. Reagan (Athens: Ohio University Press, 1979). I am also indebted to David Pellauer for guidance in the Ricoeur bibliography.

Ricoeur's own enigmatic call for *"a post-Hegelian Kantianism."*[3] The reader of Ricoeur will have experienced the tug of each of these as a way of construing the Ricoeurian unity. But here once again the writings are problematic by their very richness: how are we to relate the three? to which accord the primacy?

My aim in the present section is to suggest that we may come to understand each of these alternatives in its legitimacy and in its limitations, if we see each as springing from a distinct feature of Ricoeur's abiding method or style. The term "abiding" is determinative here: we intend a level of method sufficiently *pervasive* that it informs the entirety of the author's work, regardless of whether the enterprise of the moment be billed as phenomenology, hermeneutics or whatever. Because each feature is pervasive, because it can appear at any point, there is justification for the construction of Ricoeur which springs from it; it bids fair to account for the entirety of his work. And yet, by the same token, each approach is limited: it is relativized by the fact that other features, generating other ways of construing Ricoeur, are equally pervasive as well.

These pervasive features have been described by Don Ihde, whose account I adopt with some modifications.[4] The features may be thought of as three characteristic "moves" which Ricoeur makes variously in a variety of contexts. The first Ihde calls a "weighted focus" upon the role of the existent subject; time and again in Ricoeur's philosophy the underlying, generative activity of the human subject provides the fundamental point of reference. It is this first characteristic move which justifies the construing of Ricoeur's thought as a form of phenomenology. The second move then introduces, over against the phenomenological starting point, a "counter-focus," an alternative point of view. In Ricoeur's early work this counter-position is commonly represented by empirical science, but arguably this is also the appropriate context in which to understand Ricoeur's subsequent turn toward hermeneutics, particularly his mounting insistence upon the necessity of a certain "distanciation." Finally, having delineated position and counter-position, Ricoeur will classically seek to mediate the two, without collapsing them into one; he will postulate a third term, a limit idea reflecting an eschatologically postponed synthesis. The exact nature of this mediation is a matter of some uncertainty, but whatever its content, it is effectively represented by the call for "a post-Hegelian Kantianism."

An overview of the sort attempted here is not, it should be remembered, a recipe. It is merely a diagnostic device which may serve to highlight certain

---

[3] Ricoeur, *Confict of Interpretations*, p. 412; Ricoeur borrows the phrase from Eric Weil.

[4] See Ihde, *Hermeneutic Phenomenology*, pp. 14ff. My differences with Ihde have largely to do with the placement of Ricoeur's turn to hermeneutics. As evidence of the persistence of the three features in Ricoeur's recent thought, see his article, "Naming God," *Union Seminary Quarterly Review* 34 (1979): 219–20.

typical moments within the total movement of an author's thought. With this in mind, let us look more closely at each of the indicated moves. As the first represents Ricoeur's appropriation of Kant's Copernican revolution, it may be termed the *critical* move. The knowing, willing subject plays an irreducible role in the constitution of meaning, and thus a naive objectivism is finally meaningless: this in essence is the argument Ricoeur offers repeatedly responding to various forms of reductionism. The origins of this reasoning are found in Kant, but the move draws its immediate inspiration from the phenomenology of Edmund Husserl, specifically from the concept of a noetic-noematic correlation. It is this correlation which keeps Ricoeur's refutation of objectivism from ricocheting into an equally untenable subjectivism. So insistent is Ricoeur upon this correlation that he lays it down as a rule that the quasi-subjective, "noetic" pole is never to be approached directly, by simple introspection—but only by way of a disciplined, structural account of the quasi-objective, "noematic" given.

Thus Ricoeur's first move cannot be dismissed as a simple appeal to subjectivity. It demands a certain indirectness, hence a certain comprehensiveness—and hence the interpreter may adopt it as the key to the entirety of the author's work. Mightn't it be that the effect of Ricoeur's hermeneutical turn is simply to bestow upon the symbol (and subsequently upon metaphor and narrative) the role originally defined as that of the noematic given? If so, it would be possible to contend that his much-discussed linguistic turn is really a secondary modification, still contained within the framework of a modified phenomenology. Certainly there are a number of counterbalancing moves within Ricoeur's thought, but the weighted focus remains, after all, the weighted focus. Ricoeur himself speaks of "the graft of the hermeneutic problem onto the phenomenological method": by implication the trunk remains phenomenological.[5] This, then, is the first way of construing the nature of the Ricoeurian center.

The second move, the counter-focus, grows in importance in the course of Ricoeur's development; it comes to represent nothing less than "a second Copernican revolution," which is necessitated by the shortcomings of the first. Specifically Ricoeur holds that a counter-focus is necessary in order to establish the *receptivity* of the knowing subject; and his sense of the urgency of this point grows apace with his reservations regarding the Husserlian phenomenology.[6] The first, critical turn was effective in dispelling the naiveté of objectivism; but Ricoeur worries that the very success of this initial move may occasion "a second-level naiveté—the naiveté of criticism which consists in considering the 'transcendental,' the 'constitutive,' as the absolutely irreducible." In this manner "the 'vanity' of the ego is stretched like a veil

[5] Ricoeur, *Conflict of Interpretations*, p. 3.

[6] This point is central to Bourgeois's exposition; see his *Extension of Ricoeur's Hermeneutic*, pp. 4, 131.

over the very being of its own existence," creating "the illusion that philosophy could be a reflection without a spiritual discipline (*ascèse*), without a purification of its own seeing."[7]

At stake is the inveterate tendency of the subject "to posit itself." The determination to counter an inflated view of the subject is absolutely consistent throughout Ricoeur's career. In *Freedom and Nature* he warns that, entranced by the critical posture, "the self becomes detached and exiles itself into what the Stoics have already called the circularity of the soul. . . ."[8] In like fashion, he closes the preface to the recent collection of studies in his thought by cautioning that truth is not attained by "a Promethean act of taking a position on the self by the self and of adequation of the self to the self."[9] There is no mistaking the moral intensity which informs Ricoeur's position at this point; and the theologically oriented reader may well associate the self-enclosed ego with Luther's *cor curvum in se*, the very definition of human arrogance and sin. Once the issue has been cast in these prophetic terms, it seems inevitable that Ricoeur's reading of phenomenology should necessitate a radical reconstruction of his method. This would be the turn to hermeneutics: for as Ricoeur declares emphatically, "*listening excludes founding oneself.*"[10] And he has posed the programmatic question, "how can philosophical reflection be articulated upon the hermeneutics of symbols?"[11] By implication the base is hermeneutical. This, then, is the second answer to the question of the Ricoeurian center.

The third move, the postponed synthesis, is at once the easiest to affirm and the hardest to interpret. By reason of its comprehensiveness it seems the indisputable key to Ricoeur's position; yet the moment we venture beyond the bare formula in order to give the synthesis content, we find we have only succeeded in reopening the question of the relative importance of the moves that went before. And on that vexed question the commentators themselves are in disagreement. The thrust of Don Ihde's able exposition is to show that even in his more recent thought Ricoeur's philosophy remains, in some extended sense, a phenomenology; whereas the aim of Patrick Bourgeois's equally fine study is to argue that even in its earliest phase Ricoeur's approach is already implicitly hermeneutical. Indeed the very titles are revealing: Ihde speaks of a *Hermeneutic Phenomenology*—"phenomenology" remains the substantive—whereas Bourgeois postulates an *Extension of Ricoeur's Hermeneutic.*[12]

---

[7] Ricoeur, *Husserl: An Analysis of His Phenomenology,* trans. Edward G. Ballard and Lester E. Embree (Evanston: Northwestern University Press, 1967), pp. 228, 232; quoted by Ihde, p. 18. I am following Ihde closely at this point.

[8] Ricoeur, *Freedom and Nature,* p. 14; quoted by Ihde, p. 19.

[9] Reagan, *Studies,* p. xix.

[10] Ricoeur, "Naming God," p. 219.

[11] Ricoeur, *Conflict of Interpretations,* p. 287; emphasis altered.

[12] Cf. Ricoeur's discussion in "Phenomenology and Hermeneutics," *Nous* 11, no. 1 (1975):

Nevertheless the notion of a postponed synthesis does succeed in point-
ing up a distinct and utterly characteristic feature of Ricoeur's thought.
There is no surer rule for reading Ricoeur than to watch for the apparent
dichotomies and then to look for the arguments by which the dichotomies
will be overcome. Mary Schaldenbrand contends that common to all of
Ricoeur's writings "is this theme: imagining mediates oppositions." Thus
she finds the "pivot" of his thinking in the role of the metaphoric imagination, captured in the formula "kinship through conflict."[13] In similar fashion one might hold that the consistent thread in Ricoeur is the process of
overcoming estrangement. Overcoming the estrangement of objectivism,
overcoming the estrangement of self-enclosure: quite arguably this is the
common impetus of both the previous moves. From these suggestions it
follows that the best characterization of Ricoeur might be to see him as a
mediating thinker, mediating even between the unity of the envisioned synthesis and the diversity occasioned by its postponement. In the present essay
I associate this feature of Ricoeur's work with what I shall call his Christian humanism; and I shall argue that it is indeed central to his thought, for
better and for worse.

At the same time it must be recognized that each of the moves we have
described delimits the others, and thus each calls into question the finality
of the summations of Ricoeur which the others have engendered. The very
notion of a "weighted focus," for example, implies its own primacy; it will
not readily yield to other perspectives as if they were of equal importance.
Moreover Ricoeur is, as Robert Solomon remarks, "a passionate philosopher."[14] We saw as much ourselves in connection with the second
Ricoeurian move—but then there followed the third move, which made the
second seem only provisional. Thus it remains questionable whether we
have yet found our way to a standpoint capable of doing equal justice to the
breadth of Ricoeur's thought *and* to the passion which underlies it.

II

The problem in understanding Ricoeur has always been the peculiar
angularity of his vision regarding phenomenology and hermeneutics. One
senses that he handles these disciplines gingerly. The reason, I now wish to
suggest, is that Ricoeur has always retained a certain dissatisfaction with
these disciplines—or in any event, with some widespread interpretations of
them. We have already touched upon his critique of phenomenology; not
unrelated to this, I believe, is his vigorous and repeated dissent from the

---

85–102.

[13] Mary Schaldenbrand, "Metaphoric Imagination: Kinship through Conflict" in Reagan,
Studies, pp. 60, 79; cf. Ricoeur's response in the preface, p. xv.

[14] Robert Solomon, "Paul Ricoeur on Passion and Emotion" in Reagan, *Studies,* p. 2.

Romanticist tradition in heremenetics.[15] But what common thread connects these dissatisfactions? A clue may perhaps be found in the critical commonplace that the Romanticist tradition, which has been so central to modern hermeneutics, has looked upon interpretation as a process of discerning the supernatural within the natural, the infinite in the finite.[16]

The infinite in the finite: the phrase recalls the *finitum capax infiniti*, "the finite is capable of the infinite," the classic Lutheran touchstone for discussions of Christology and the sacraments. Isn't it possible that a contemporary debate over hermeneutics and phenomenology, symbol and subjectivity, might echo an earlier struggle over sacrament and person? And isn't it plausible, in such a case, that Ricoeur's own position might be closer to the classical Calvinist dictum, *finitum non capax infiniti*, "the finite is not capable of the infinite"? The hypothesis then would be, in simplest terms, that one might understand Ricoeur as a Calvinist working within, and to some extent against, a broadly Lutheran tradition. Admittedly it is something of a leap to characterize phenomenology and hermeneutics, even on Ricoeur's distinctive view, as Lutheran media; that will take some arguing. But what is attractive about the notion is that by construing Ricoeur's coherence in terms of this tension, indeed perhaps this contradiction, it makes intelligible his dynamic, the open-endedness of his thought. The proposal might thus provide a way of addressing the very phenomenon which has perplexed the other approaches to the Ricoeurian center, namely the interplay of currents and crosscurrents in his work, the restlessness and elusiveness of the ever-unfolding project.

The proposal must be understood, however, in such a way as not to obscure the fact that Ricoeur's work is that of a philosopher, albeit a philosopher who has reflected upon religious symbols. As Ricoeur himself has cautioned, "the philosopher is not a preacher. He may listen to preaching, as I do; but insofar as he is a professional and responsible thinker, he remains a beginner, and his discourse always remains a preparatory discourse."[17] The terms "Calvinist" and "Lutheran" as used in the present discussion are simply a conceptual shorthand for two possible ways of relating the finite and the infinite. Certainly the philosophical positions are analogous to the classic theological options; they may indeed have, to use Ricoeur's term, a certain "preparatory" significance for the doing of theology; and the theological connotations may suggest why the finite/infinite issue could be for Ricoeur a matter of passionate importance. But none of this alters the fact that within the present context the two options are conceived in strictly philosophical terms. Related to this matter of clarification is a further point,

---

[15] See, e.g., Ricoeur, *Interpretation Theory*, pp. 22–23.
[16] See, e.g., M. H. Abrams, *Natural Supernaturalism: Tradition and Revolution in Romantic Literature* (New York: W. W. Norton & Co., 1971), pp. 65–70.
[17] Ricoeur, *Conflict of Interpretations*, pp. 441.

having to do with the genetic fallacy. It happens that Ricoeur's own background has in fact been informed by the French Calvinist tradition. But this
is a biographical datum which, for our purposes, can be no more than a
"diagnostic" clue. That is to say, following Ricoeur's exposition of the
diagnostic in *Freedom and Nature*, it is a consideration drawn from one mode
of inquiry which may be suggestive to a person pursuing another mode of
inquiry—but which, once suggested, must then be justified solely in the
terms of the second mode of inquiry.[18] Biography, in the end, proves nothing; the Calvinist and Lutheran paradigms must be judged solely by their
powers as a typology: by their ability to illumine Ricoeur's thought not as
regards its accidental origins but as regards its inherent structure, its inner
movement and its aim.

These cautions duly posted, we may be able to take a further step without inviting confusion. So long as they remain defined in terms of a single
issue, the Calvinist and Lutheran paradigms must seem rather one-
dimensional. But it is possible to discern within each an internal tension
and thus an internal dynamic. To do this we must take our clue once again
from historic Calvinism and Lutheranism. We need to delineate in these
historic movements certain further features which might possibly be
reflected—analogously—within the premises of Ricoeur's philosophy. Let us
begin with the *finitum non capax* of historic Calvinism. It has been of course
an affirmation of the transcendence and sovereignty of God. But taken by
itself this insistence can lead to a dualism, a form of Manichaeanism, as
indeed it has at times within the Calvinist tradition. For just this reason,
however, Calvinism itself has generated a countervailing force which served
to mitigate this initial harshness. It was not, certainly, a simple notion of
immanence; that would have been too flat a contradiction. Rather it was
what one might term a characteristic Calvinist humanism. This tendency,
evident in Calvin's own adherence to certain premises of his classical education, was perpetuated in a Calvinist optimism epitomized in certain notions
of sanctification. What makes this development intriguing is that the
countervailing force does not simply reflect the covert importation of a
properly Lutheran theme. Indeed the notions of classical humanism and
progressive sanctification are at least as antithetical to the Lutheran stance as
is the *finitum non capax*. The remedy is a homegrown antibody which has
endowed historic Calvinism with a peculiar complexity and dynamic.
Accordingly, we shall wish to ask whether Ricoeur may not have introduced into his philosophy in one fashion or another, appropriately or
inappropriately, the "preparatory" concerns of a Christian humanist.

Turning to the Lutheran side, one finds a comparable phenomenon.
Taken by itself the *finitim capax* would suggest an immanentalism; and

---

[18] See Ricoeur, *Freedom and Nature*, p. 13; regarding certain ambiguities in Ricoeur's use of
this notion, see Ihde, pp. 29-32.

indeed a good deal has been made of the links between Luther and a certain mystical tradition. But within Luther's own thought such tendencies were never permitted to divorce themselves from the centrality of the cross; and the suffering of the cross, whatever else it may signify, must embody conflict and contradiction. Accordingly, it may be important to attend to the relative presence or absence of an analogous notion of conflict within Ricoeur's philosophy.

Now, with this amplified typology in hand, let us see what can be made of the peculiar course of Ricoeur's development. In the 1940s when Ricoeur began his *Philosophy of the Will*, the existentialism of Jean-Paul Sartre was in the ascendency; and it is not stretching the point to say that Ricoeur regarded this form of existentialism as a contemporary Manichaeanism. We may leave to the student of French literature the implication that Sartre may represent one side of Calvin run rampant; what is certain is that the Sartrean position offended not only Ricoeur's general religious convictions, as regards for example the existence of God, but quite specifically his Christian humanism. As Ricoeur recalls in a retrospective essay, "My problem was to distinguish between finitude and guilt. I had the impression, or even the conviction, that these two terms tended to be identified in classical existentialism at the cost of both experiences, guilt becoming a particular case of finitude and for that reason beyond cure and forgiveness, and finitude, on the other hand, being affected by a kind of diffused sense of sadness and despair through guilt."[19] To alleviate this situation Ricoeur adopted a strategy which was to prove typical of his thought: he would take up the challenge on his opponent's own terms; he would dispute Sartre on the grounds of phenomenology. Thus in *Freedom and Nature Ricoeur argued on the basis* of a more ample phenomenology that the two terms of the title, freedom and nature (or the "for itself" and the "in itself" of Sartre), are not so fundamentally antagonistic. Rather Ricoeur's persistent theme, patiently traced through numerous strata of human experience, is that the voluntary and the involuntary exhibit themselves as positively interdependent; to put it metaphorically, human willing would be powerless were it not for the traction provided by the resistant, involuntary aspects of our experience. In this fashion Ricoeur's philosophy serves the interests of a Christian humanism; and it does so, we should note, by surmounting certain dichotomies—by a process of mediation.

But the instrument Ricoeur had adopted to accomplish this end was, specifically, a form of Husserlian phenomenology; and that philosophy, Ricoeur increasingly came to believe, was deeply implicated in the effort to become a philosophy without presuppositions, a philosophy which would

---

[19] Paul Ricoeur, "From Existentialism to the Philosophy of Language," *Philosophy Today* 17, no. 2/4 (1973): 89. The contrast with Sartre is elaborated by David Stewart in "Existential Humanism," in Reagan, *Studies*, pp. 22–32.

found itself. To Ricoeur this philosophic enterprise seemed the very paradigm of the subject circling upon itself, the penchant toward self-enclosure.
Translated into our typology, the transcendental ego of phenomenology
represented an effort to locate the infinite within the finite. In this light it
becomes possible to discern a neglected aspect of Ricoeur's turn toward
hermeneutics. That turn was intended not simply *to supplement* what could
be accomplished by phenomenology: it was also intended *to set limits to* that
philosophy. By thrusting upon philosophic discourse the symbol, with its
inexhaustible multivalency of meaning, Ricoeur consciously introduced an
object which by its very density must curtail the pretensions of human
reflection. The claims of reflection were relativized, and the claim to self-
sufficiency was negated altogether.[20] Thus one reason for the turn from the
straightforward phenomenology of *Freedom and Nature* to the hermeneutics
of *The Symbolism of Evil* was Ricoeur's determination to forestall the peculiar
confidence in the *finitum capax* which, historically, had contributed to German idealism. This point needs stressing because it is easy to suppose that
Ricoeur's turn to the symbol (and subsequently to metaphor, parable and
narrative) was prompted solely by a Romanticist zeal for the fullness of
language, a quasi-aesthetic attraction to the richness of symbolic discourse.
We shall return to that skewed reading of Ricoeur in the course of our
final section; for the present let us give full weight to Ricoeur's own profes-
sion that he resorted to hermeneutics not in order to recapture a lost, first
naiveté but as a second-order move: to criticize the critical spirit of modern
times.[21]

It may be helpful now to pause a moment to review. The polemic
against Sartre was prompted by one side of what we have characterized as
Ricoeur's Calvinism, namely his Christian humanism. But the *method*

---

[20] More recently the multivalency of the symbol has given way to the "polyphonic" character of Biblical discourse. The task of setting limits, however, remains constant. Ricoeur
cautions, for example, that "the amalgamation of Being and God is the most subtle seduc-
tion." He invokes Kant and then proceeds to relate Biblical polyphony to "the paralogisms
and antinomies" which "become for critical reason the ascetic instruments by which it is led
back to itself within those boundaries where its knowledge is valid" ("Naming God," p. 219).
Ricoeur's Kantianism is to a large extent interchangeable with what I am calling a
Calvinist insistence upon the *finitum non capax*. But once he has made the classic Kantian
move, Ricoeur characteristically proceeds to a "second reflection," inspired by Gabriel Marcel
and Jean Nabert, which criticizes critical reason and opens the way for a certain guarded
ontology. Thus the questions presently under discussion might be reformulated by asking: is
this second move best understood as still being critical and Kantian, in some extended
sense—a matter of being more Kantian than Kant? Or is it rather a *reversal* of Kant, as the
reappearance of ontology would suggest? And most basically: what is the consistent purpose
which would hold together this entire series of moves and countermoves?

[21] Ricoeur, *Symbolism of Evil*, p. 352. In an acute discussion of Bultmann, that arch-
representative of the critical spirit, Ricoeur argues contra Bultmann that "the act of God has
its first transcendence in the objectivity of meaning which it announces for us" (*Conflict of
Interpretations*, p. 398).

Ricoeur adopted in this debate became itself, in turn, a source of difficulty. For Husserlian phenomenology—on Ricoeur's reading of it, we must always remember—was inconsistent with the other face of the Calvinist position, the *finitum non capax*. Thus by what is almost an internal logic, Ricoeur's thought was driven to a further stage, designed as an implicit critique of phenomenology; and that stage, as we have seen, is his turn to hermeneutics.

Such has been our account. But if there is merit in this reading of Ricoeur, a further development seems well-nigh inevitable. For hermeneutics was able to function as a check against the presumption of human reflection by virtue of the inexhaustible richness of the symbol; and in light of our initial comment about the influence of Romanticism upon modern hermeneutics, it is clear that discovering the depth of symbolic discourse may become a further occasion for asserting the *finitum capax*. What better evidence of the infinite in the finite than the celebrative self-transcendence expressed and embodied in mythic-symbolic language? Ricoeur himself seems to promise as much when he introduces hermeneutics as the antidote to a modern consciousness which has fallen into a state of forgetfulness: "forgetting hierophanies, forgetting the signs of the Sacred, losing hold of man himself as belonging to the Sacred."[22] Thus the earlier logic repeats itself. Once again the instrument which Ricoeur adopted to resolve one set of problems becomes, in its own turn, problematical. To put it roughly, just as the Husserlian phenomenology embodied the *finitum capax* from the side of the subject, in the transcendental ego, so now a Romanticist hermeneutic asserts the *finitum capax* from the side of the object, in the inexhaustible symbol—an infinite presumably graspable in a moment of intuitive apprehension.

Once again, therefore, a corrective is required; to secure it Ricoeur addresses the last point, the notion of an intuitive apprehension. Here we may have a key to the more recent turn in Ricoeur's development, the turn *within* Ricoeur's hermeneutical studies from the relatively straightforward discussions found in *The Symbolism of Evil* to the more dialectical approach exemplified by his work on psychoanalysis and structuralist linguistics. Ricoeur makes it clear that the aim of these various inquiries is to expose the naiveté of the common appeals to intuition or introspection. What is required instead is a detour—by way of a certain "archeology" in the case of psychoanalysis, by way of structural analysis in the case of linguistics—a longer path or, in Ricoeur's familiar terminology, a necessary *distanciation*, a purification or a discipline.[23] But with this notion of discipline, of a spiritual *ascèse*, we are returned to the themes of Ricoeur's earlier critique of Husserl.

---

[22] Ricoeur, *Conflict of Interpretations*, p. 288.

[23] For a discussion of Ricoeur's insistence upon distanciation and his consequent disagreement with Gadamer, see David Pellauer, "The Significance of the Text in Paul Ricoeur's Hermeneutical Theory" in Reagan, *Studies*, pp. 106–8.

Thus it is possible to contend that even now, in this most recent phase of Ricoeur's development, we are dealing with the issue of the *finitum capax*.

In the end, the hypothesis we have been entertaining must stand or fall on the basis of its ability to deal with the enigma of Ricoeur's development: from the launching of the *Philosophy of the Will* to the shift to hermeneutics, still within the parameters of that project; and then to the further hermeneutical shift out of the anticipated framework of the *Philosophy of the Will* and into a succession of encounters with psychoanalysis, linguistics, and literary criticism. Ricoeur himself has recently avowed, "it is difficult for me to see my books and articles as steps or stages in a single development. Each seems to be rather a response to a particular question determined by the questions left unanswered in the preceding work."[24] The effect of our present inquiry is to acknowledge that Ricoeur's writings may indeed be a series of responses to problems left unresolved (and even occasioned!) by the work that went before—and yet to argue that nevertheless the writings do constitute "a single development," in the sense that they elaborate and defend a distinct position which is recurrent, if not abstractly consistent. In lieu of abstract consistency, the typology views Ricoeur's thought as being shaped by a two-fold tension: first a tension internal to Calvinism as such, and then the further tension occasioned by the decision to work with, and against, a certain "Lutheran" tradition. These tensions once posited, Ricoeur's development displays an internal logic which seems to unfold of its own accord: from the initial adoption of phenomenology, to the critique of (Husserlian) phenomenology by the subsequent adoption of hermeneutics, and thence to the most recent critique of (Romanticist) hermeneutics.

III

Fallible Man, Ricoeur's unduly neglected exercise in philosophical anthropology, sought to delineate the peculiar restlessness which seems inherent in the human makeup. The source and center of that tension he called the human "heart" or, borrowing from Plato, the *thumos*.[25] In analogous fashion the present paper may be said to be seeking the *thumos* of Ricoeur's own thought. The question, raised in the first section, was addressed in the second section by an ad hoc typology. In this final section I attempt to assess the typology, to draw some conclusions regarding the original question of the Ricoeurian center and to offer a few remarks toward an assessment of Ricoeur's own thought.

On the strength of the foregoing exposition it may be claimed that the

---

[24] Ricoeur, "Preface" to Reagan, *Studies*, pp. xiv–xv.

[25] See Ricoeur, *Fallible Man*, pp. 161–91; the theme is examined at length in Lowe, *Mystery & the Unconscious: A Study in the Thought of Paul Ricoeur* (Metuchen, NJ: Scarecrow Press, 1977), pp. 59–82.

theme of the *finitum non capax* does seem to point up a significant aspect of Ricoeur's position. It is, moreover, an aspect which is apt to be neglected. To illustrate, I must note that the use of the Calvinist/Lutheran thematic as a way of construing Ricoeur is not original with the present essay. Ron C. Alexander alluded to these categories in the closing lines of an article published in 1975. What is striking, however, is that Alexander arrives at a very different conclusion: he holds that "instead of embracing the Calvinistic dictum, *finitum non capax infiniti*, Ricoeur will have to give up and embrace the Lutheran dictum, *finitum capax infiniti*. After all, the whole of his philosophy seems to focus time and again on the capacity of the finite containing the infinite."[26] I hope the present inquiry has succeeded in showing that there is more in Ricoeur than such a conclusion would allow. And yet we must ask whether Alexander's insistence upon the *finitum capax* is not significant in that it reflects something of the perspective which is commonly brought to Ricoeur, particularly by those in religious studies. Are we not drawn to Ricoeur because of his rebuttals of various reductionist opponents? Do we not come to him already more or less committed to the Romanticist project of discerning the supernatural within the natural? And is it not possible that, coming at Ricoeur with these preoccupations, we may miss something which is central to what he has to say?[27]

This returns us to the question of the Ricoeurian center. If we acknowledge the *finitum non capax* as a necessary and irreducible *element* within his thought, what can we say more positively and more comprehensively about the aim or telos of his work? I would suggest that Ricoeur's positive vision is expressed in his early work by a concept of "mystery" drawn from Gabriel Marcel, and in his more recent hermeneutical work by the question of Being and the concept of "being-in-the-world" drawn from Martin Heidegger.[28] In both cases Ricoeur insists that the crucial end point be approached indirectly, by way of a longer path; this is a theme we have learned to anticipate. What is less evident is that, when they are properly understood, a certain indirectness is built into the concepts themselves. The Marcellian concept of mystery presupposes certain antinomies: for example, the fact that I experience my body both as a neutral, observable object and

---

[26] Ronald G. Alexander, "Paul Ricoeur: What Direction is He Taking?," *Dialog* 14, no. 1 (1975): 61. Alexander's own typology is to view Ricoeur as a theological Barthian. On this premise one could readily understand why there might be certain tensions in Ricoeur's thought, but it becomes difficult to explain why such a person would have chosen to write a philosophical anthropology in the first place.

[27] Even so able a commentator as Mary Schaldenbrand frames Ricoeur's significance in terms of this issue, the overcoming of positivism ("Metaphoric Imagination," pp. 79–80). The issue is undoubtedly of great importance, but problems arise when it becomes a preoccupation; cf. the Introduction to the present volume.

[28] See Ricoeur, *Freedom and Nature*, p. 15; *Conflict of Interpretations*, pp. 6–7.

as the "lived body." But the concept of mystery is *not* set forth as a Romanticist advocacy of the ineffability of the lived body *over* the objectivism of science. Rather, to adopt a phrase from H. J. Blackham, the mystery of existence is to be sought in "the mid-region between" the various antinomies.[29] Thus, however the particular antinomies be conceived, the crucial point in each case is that one keep one's attention trained upon "the midregion between"—and not be drawn away by the phantasm of some transcendent or infinite beyond. This point is difficult to make in the abstract; it is even more difficult to accomplish in practice. But the effort to do so is, I think, constitutive of the telos of Ricoeur's philosophy.

Once we grasp something of this vision, we are in a position to come to a judgment about the significance and the limits of the *finitum non capax*. For in the end I believe that Ricoeur would find even so pointed an issue as the *finitum non capax* versus the *finitum capax* to be an unacceptable disjunction. In effect one side of Ricoeur's Calvinism, the *finitum non capax*, would eventually be relativized—not by a borrowed Lutheranism, but by the other side of the Calvinist paradigm: namely, the role of the Christian humanist, which Ricoeur takes to be the role of the mediating thinker. Accordingly, the Marcellian concept of mystery, the Heideggerian "being-in-the-world" and even (as Ricoeur notes almost incidentally) the late Husserlian "lived experience"—all of these have their significance in that they enable Ricoeur to mediate this very disjunction.[30] In briefest terms, it happens as follows. Ricoeur's position as I understand it is that the infinite or the transcendent does indeed contribute to the constitution of the mid-region, of our being-in-the-world. In the Kantian terms for which *Fallible Man* prepares us, the infinite is a condition of the possibility of that reality. This Ricoeur would affirm as the philosophic truth of the *finitum capax*. But the role of that infinite is properly exhausted in the task of constituting; and thus it is never possible for us to encounter the presence of the infinite directly. At most it might be approached in an act of appresentation. This quasi-Kantian limitation is what we repeatedly forget in our repeated efforts to grasp the infinite in, through or beyond the realm of mystery. Accordingly there is constant need of a brusque reminder, a summons to the discipline of attention; and this is the abiding philosophic truth of the *finitum non capax*.[31]

In this assiduously balanced position it seems to me that we have Ricoeur at his best. In effect we have Ricoeur using his offices as a mediating thinker in order to transcend the type in which we had placed him.

---

[29] H. J. Blackham, *Six Existentialist Thinkers* (New York: Harper Torchbooks, 1959), p. 72; cf. Ricoeur, *Fallible Man*, pp. 5-6.

[30] Paul Ricoeur, "Philosophical Hermeneutics and Theological Hermeneutics," *Studies in Religion/Sciences Religieuses* 5, no. 1 (1975): 25.

[31] Regarding appresentation, see Edward Farley, *Ecclesial Man: A Social Phenomenology of Faith and Reality* (Philadelphia: Fortress Press, 1975), pp. 194ff. Regarding the Kantian critique of false consciousness, see Ricoeur, *Freud and Philosophy*, pp. 529-30.

Or, to reaffirm the typology from another angle: we have Ricoeur demonstrating that it is no accident that this "Calvinist" should elect to achieve his ends through specifically "Lutheran" means. Had we space enough and time, we might examine how this fuller understanding of Ricoeur's telos permits a more ample account of his development: from the Marcellian mystery of the body in *Freedom and Nature* to the Marcellian mystery of evil in *The Symbolism of Evil*, and thence to the Heideggerian concept of being-in-the-world in the most recent hermeneutical writings. In each case we would wish to show how the central concept functions to overcome an inadequate understanding of the finite *and of the infinite*. A fulcral point in this two-fold polemic would be the way the concepts in question aim to surmount a narcissism of the spirit and to assure a certain human receptivity. The theme of receptivity has been underlined by Patrick Bourgeois; it is consistent throughout the vicissitudes of Ricoeur's development. As early as *Freedom and Nature* he held that "within the human will there is inscribed a particular receptivity which one has no right to confuse with a simple passivity."[32] And in a recent study in hermeneutics he speaks warmly of the power of the text to bestow a Self—"by Self I mean a non-egoistic, non-narcissistic, non-imperialistic mode of subjectivity which responds and corresponds to the power of a work to display a *world*."[33]

If these remarks suggest something of Ricoeur's intent, it only remains to ask how successfully he accomplishes it. Ricoeur at his best, I believe we can say, is trying to do what Heidegger was doing, and more. He is trying to address the Heideggerian "question of Being," but to do so by a longer, more comprehensive path.[34] In practice, however, it would seem that the concept of "being-in-the-world," whose centrality to Ricoeur we have just remarked, effectively preempts the place of the larger question. It is almost as if Ricoeur assumed that the question of Being, the fundamental question of Heidegger's thought, were sufficiently addressed by a delineation of our being-in-the-world. That such is not the case Heidegger himself increasingly came to realize; and so Ricoeur's philosophy must be said to remain, from the Heideggerian viewpoint, a regional ontology. The rationale for this restriction lies with a phenomenon we have observed consistently throughout our discussion: the fact that Ricoeur's thought is consistently oriented, *whether positively or negatively*, to a certain concept of "the Self."[35] In

---

[32] Paul Ricoeur, *The Philosophy of Paul Ricoeur: An Anthology of His work*, ed. Charles E. Reagan and David Stewart (Boston: Beacon Press, 1978), p. 6. This volume is extraordinarily useful in that it includes essays which represent Ricoeur's own précis of a number of his major works. Some of the reprinted essays have been abridged.

[33] Ricoeur, "Philosophical Hermeneutics," p. 30; emphasis Ricoeur's.

[34] See Ricoeur, *The Conflict of Interpretations*, pp. 6–11; idem, *The Rule of Metaphor*, pp. 309–13.

[35] See, e.g., Ricoeur "Philosophical Hermeneutics," p. 31; though cf. "Heidegger and the Question of the Subject," in *Conflict of Interpretations*, pp. 223–35.

other words, Ricoeur is oriented less to ontology than to philosophical anthropology, less to the problem of truth than to the question of human meaningfulness; and between these respective issues there are important differences, as Ricoeur's Lonerganian critics have been quick to recognize.[36]

Ricoeur's philosophy remains a regional ontology; or, in the terminology of Heidegger's letter to Jean Beaufret, it remains a "humanism."[37] The term "humanism" recalls the typology once again; and I believe the association is to the point, for the typology may cast some further light on the present quandary. I think Ricoeur is correct in judging that nothing short of the full Heideggerian concept of Being will enable him to achieve his own telos regarding the relation of the *finitum capax* and the *finitum non capax*. But Ricoeur is barred from entering fully into the Heideggerian project because of his, Ricoeur's, particular interpretation of the responsibilities of the Christian humanist. In effect Ricoeur is prevented from his goal of radically *relativizing* human subjectivity because his very method persists in retaining a weighted focus on the *significance for* that same subjectivity.

Perhaps, in conclusion, our inquiry may also suggest a way in which this deadlock might be surmounted. The possibility would be for Ricoeur to embrace more fully the remaining element of the typology, the other face of the Lutheran position—the element of conflict. For all the references in Ricoeur's writings to dialectic and conflict, the presiding image for his method remains that of an ellipse; his thought remains a mediating philosophy.[38] In the study of Freud, for example, "archeology" and "teleology" are presented as a cardinal instance of "the conflict of interpretations." But of the two, teleology is accorded a certain preeminence, it becomes the inclusive term; and thus beyond the conflict we glimpse an immanent resolution.[39] To

---

[36] See Peter Joseph Albano, *Freedom, Truth and Hope: The Relationship of Philosophy and Religion in the Thought of Paul Ricoeur* (Ann Arbor: University Microfilms, 1976), pp. 159–70; see also Ted Peters, "The Problem of Symbolic Reference," *The Thomist* 44, no. 1 (1980): 72–93; and cf. Klaus Hartmann's extensive critique of Ricoeur's *Philosophy of the Will*, "Phenomenology, Ontology and Metaphysics," *The Review of Metaphysics* 22, no. 1 (1968): 81–112. The elements of a corrective may be found in *The Rule of Metaphor*, particularly in the remarkable concluding chapter with its robust defense of the prerogatives of speculative philosophy. For a review essay highlighting this aspect of the book, which must come as a surprise to those who had assumed that for Ricoeur the last word was the irreducibly metaphorical character of language, see Mary Gerhart, "*La métaphore vive* by Paul Ricoeur," *Religious Studies Review* 2, no. 1 (1976): 23–30; also her "The Extent and Limits of Metaphor: Reply to Gary Madison," *Philosophy Today* 21, no. 4/4 (1977): 431–36.

[37] See Martin Heidegger, *Basic Writings*, ed. David Farrell Krell (New York: Harper and Row, 1977), pp. 189–242.

[38] The figure of an ellipse is drawn from Ihde, who uses it, however, to a contrary effect (Ihde, *Hermeneutic Phenomenology*, p. 16).

[39] This criticism is argued at length in Chapter One above. Ihde acknowledges that "Hegel inverts Freud, and Ricoeur ultimately sides with Hegel" (Ihde, *Hermeneutic Phenomenology*, p. 159). Robert Solomon observes, more critically: "What emerges from *Freud and Philosophy* is a giving up of the biological side of the matter virtually altogether, and turning Freud—or

put the criticism in Heideggerian terms, Ricoeur's philosophy remains a philosophy of "presence." It does not allow for the radical interpenetration of "concealment" and "revealedness," nor for their irreducible conflict.[40]

Thus Ricoeur's own philosophy might almost be taken to illustrate the point which Heidegger would wish to make. For the truth of his philosophy seems inseparable from a conflict, the conflict between its telos and its "humanistic" precommitments; and that conflict, itself, is concealed. It follows that whatever usefulness our typology may have must be found in its capacity to lead us into that conflict, which is the source of so much of Ricoeur's thought—in its power, in its limitations, and in its inestimable value.

---

what emerges in the name of Freud—into hermeneutical and highly phenomenological product. Now this may be a way of resolving the central antinomy in Freud's theories. . . . But it does not do what Ricoeur most wants it to do, and that is to preserve both moments in the 'third term'" (Solomon, "Paul Ricoeur," pp. 12-13).

[40] An adequate treatment of this issue in Ricoeur would require a close study of his relationship to Husserl. Bourgeois prepares the way in discussing "the status of representation"; see Bourgeois, *Extension of Ricoeur's Hermeneutic*, pp. 75-79, 99-102.

CHAPTER THREE
PSYCHOANALYSIS AND HUMANISM

> The level which a science has reached
> is determined by how far it is capable
> of a crisis in its basic concepts.
> Martin Heidegger

The theological response to psychoanalysis has been an ongoing effort to say "yes, but . . ." to Freud. In 1936, writing to Ludwig Binswanger regarding the psychoanalytic view of human experience, Freud acknowledged, "I have always lived on the ground floor and in the basement of the building."[1] This seeming admission may be taken as the charter of many subsequent critiques of Freud, whether they be broadly humanistic or specifically theological. The consistent effort has been to affirm Freud's insights but to amplify his psychology, introducing a greater appreciation of such higher aspects as freedom, value and the human search for meaning.

Now I think it is fair to say that in rejecting a Freudian reductionism which tended toward being a materialist metaphysic, most of these critiques tended toward an alternative position which was, itself, either explicitly or implicitly metaphysical. The root metaphor of this metaphysic, as the image of a many-storied mansion suggests, was predominantly hierarchical. The psychology of Abraham Maslow is an obvious example; but the model may be extended, through various stage theories of human development, to include many forms of Freudian revisionism as well. For purposes of a general typology, the various instances of this approach may be gathered under the rubric of a "humanistic" psychology.[2] It is a position which has demonstrated a powerful appeal in many areas of theology, both practical and theoretical.

---

[1] Less often cited is the context of Freud's "admission": "Of course I don't believe you. I have always lived on the ground floor and in the basement of the building—you maintain that on changing one's viewpoint one can also see an upper floor housing such distinguished guests as religion, art and others. You are not the only one; most cultivated specimens of *homo natura* think likewise. In this respect you are the conservative, I the revolutionary." Sigmund Freud, *The Letters of Sigmund Freud,* ed. Ernst L. Freud, trans. Tania Stern and James Stern (New York: Basic Books, 1960), p. 431; quoted by Russell Jacoby, *Social Amnesia: A Critique of Conformist Psychology from Adler to Laing* (Boston: Beacon Press, 1975), p. 55.

[2] A fuller characterization of "humanistic psychology" will be found under that heading below. In the present text "the humanist" is to be understood as a shorthand term referring primarily to the humanistic psychologist. Regrettably limitations of space will preclude discussion of the distinctive contribution of Carl Jung.

But already in the 1950s, Paul Tillich and Reinhold Niebuhr had voiced fundamental reservations. Tillich, for example, held that in psychologists such as Erich Fromm "we miss the depths of Freud. We miss the feeling for the irrational element that we have in Freud and in much of the existentialist literature."[3] In short, efforts at revision had too often suppressed Freud's critical edge and his tragic vision. Yet the continued popularity of humanistic approaches made it evident that the neo-orthodox dissent had gone substantially unheeded. In retrospect the reason for this theological impasse is apparent: the theologians did not yet dispose of the conceptual tools which they needed to make their criticism stick and to forge a viable alternative. As regards making the criticism stick, there was the irony that in principle the desired aspects of Freud had been affirmed and incorporated within the hierarchical framework. It would require close conceptual scrutiny to show that in practice certain features had been smothered within the commodious embrace. And as regards an alternative, the only option at hand was an existential psychology which finally proved insufficiently comprehensive—thus the further irony that the theologians themselves were driven back upon some form of the hierarchical model. On both counts the theologians found little assistance from the side of philosophy, which, particularly in the English-speaking world, remained largely aloof from any engagement with psychoanalysis.

In 1965 Paul Ricoeur's monumental study appeared under the title *De l'interprétation: Essai sur Freud*. The very title suggested a response to the theological need, the introduction of a distinctively hermeneutical framework which might afford analytic discrimination and general comprehensiveness. It soon became evident that Ricoeur had indeed shifted the grounds of the debate. In his hands the competing metaphysics, materialist and hierarchical, became alternative moments of interpretation, the "archeological" and the "teleological," and these moments were effectively contained within the larger setting which he characterized as "the conflict of interpretations."[4] The significance of this shift to hermeneutics may be measured by its effects. Hierarchy was no longer assumed as normative; it was relativized to the role of one alternative among others. Moreover the relation between the two frameworks was no longer one of subsumption; it became a dialectical interaction. And accordingly Freud's "hermeneutic of suspicion" became more than a partial insight; it attained to a positive significance in its own right. The theme of a more authentic pluralism, introduced by Ricoeur's turn to hermeneutics, was to reappear in writers as diverse as Peter Homans,

---

[3] Paul Tillich, *Theology of Culture* (New York: Oxford University Press, 1959), p. 122. Cf. Reinhold Niebuhr, "Human Creativity and Self-Concern in Freud's Thought," in *Freud and the Twentieth Century*, ed. Benjamin Nelson (New York: Meridian Books, 1957), p. 271.

[4] Paul Ricoeur, *Freud and Philosophy: An Essay on Interpretation*, trans. Denis Savage (New Haven: Yale University Press, 1970), pp. 459ff.

Don Browning and James Hillman.

In the previous chapters I have been compelled to argue, however, that just as the hierarchical-metaphysical approach is appealing in principle but inadequate in practice, so Ricoeur's own hermeneutical approach falls short of its initial vision. Now I wish to suggest that what is needed is a further extension of the reflective "detour" which Ricoeur has opened up, a further unfolding of the mediating offices of philosophy.[5] But I believe that the effect of such investigation will be to relativize the role of hermeneutics itself, by restoring the psychological discussion to its philosophic rootage in the tradition which issues from Hegel and Kant. To lay the ground for this argument, a first section will introduce a simple typology, arranged in a heuristic diagram; the purpose of this schema is simply to bring to attention certain neglected issues and themes. A second, longer section will then seek to interpret these issues by placing them in the context of transcendental philosophy, and a concluding section will offer some summary observations.

I

Let us begin by asking: what is the shape of the psychological terrain which is available to the theologian post Freud? The question stipulates that while our concerns are finally theological, the task at hand is preparatory: namely to set forth certain underlying issues which must inform any theological assessment of the options within psychology. Further, the reference to Freud stipulates that for purposes of focus, the discussion will center upon certain positions which are related, whether positively or negatively, to Freud's pioneering account of the unconscious.

The simplest access to the issues is perhaps the straightforward typology with which we began: Freudian psychoanalysis versus humanistic psychology, with the attendant contrast between a materialist and a hierarchical worldview. From this starting point one could then proceed to soften the contrast, showing for example that Freud may be reinterpreted in the direction of a more ample psychology. Thus the initial positions would become the poles of a spectrum and the task would be to fill in the options: neo-Freudians to the right, post-Freudians to the left, the entire symphony. But our aim, which is to sharpen the issues, will not be accomplished by immersing ourselves in the subtleties of an intermingling spectrum. Instead let us stick to a few ideal types, trying to tease out their inherent logic. I propose to introduce between Freudian psychoanalysis and humanistic psychology one mediating type which I shall call "existential psychology." This title suggests the thought of Martin Heidegger, but in the individual types as in the arrangement at large we must be prepared to trade subtlety

---

[5] Cf. Ricoeur, *The Conflict of Interpretations: Essays in Hermeneutics* (Evanston: Northwestern University Press, 1974), pp. 6–11.

for clarity. Thus our primary model of an existential psychology will rather be the early writings of Jean-Paul Sartre.

The addition of this third type has a prima facie plausibility if one recalls that Tillich and Niebuhr characteristically invoked existentialist themes in their effort to find an alternative to both Freudian psychoanalysis and humanistic psychology. And the resultant arrangement, with existential psychology inserted between the other two, makes sense in terms of common usage. Sartre speaks of an "existential psychoanalysis" and he has also declared that "existentialism is a humanism"—but it would be appropriately difficult to find a joining of the two extremes, a "humanistic psychoanalysis." The remainder of the present section will test this arrangement by examining the affinities and contrasts which it suggests. As an anticipatory summary, a way of construing the conceptual terrain, I propose to amplify our three-part typology by means of the following schema:

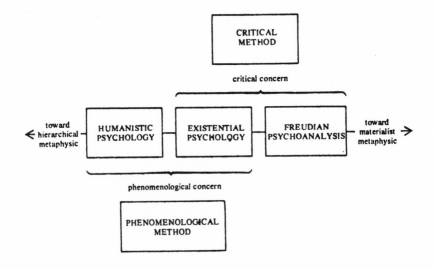

This initial schematization of the issues and themes which we shall confront may gain significance as the discussion proceeds.

A good place to begin is with the obvious affinities between humanistic psychology and existential psychology. Maslow, Allport, Rogers, and May have all endorsed the quest for an existential psychology: they are variously intent upon moving with Heidegger beyond the merely "ontic" or with Kierkegaard beyond the "aesthetic" toward the fullness of human experience.[6] Enumerating a few of the shared concerns which characterize this

---

[6] Rollo May, ed., *Existence: A New Dimension in Psychiatry and Psychology* (New York: Basic Books, 1958); idem, ed., *Existential Psychology* (New York: Random House, 1960).

alliance, we find a series of pointed contrasts to the materialist alternative. For humanistic psychologists and existential psychologists share (1) a resolve to describe phenomena in their own terms, rather than explain them in other terms. Specifically (2) both groups wish to describe in terms of meaning for an existing subject, rather than explain in terms of the causality of certain forces. All of this (3) in the context of our relational being-in-the-world, rather than in the setting of some postulated system of psychic structures. Thus the bracket to the lower left of the diagram, for concerns such as these may be spoken of as distinctively "phenomenological."

These engaging affinities have inclined many not only to connect humanistic and existential psychology, but to use the terms interchangeably. But if we acknowledge Sartre as exemplar and Heidegger as progenitor, existentialism presses upon us a further range of concerns which find little place among the commitments of humanistic psychology. For classical existentialism views the human under the sign of separation and estrangement. To speak of "the human," as the humanist so readily does, is not in fact to confer an identity—it is to expose an absence. "Existence precedes essence." The truth is that our existence is secured by no human nature, it has only a destiny; and our destiny has no goal but freedom—pointless and inescapable. We are "condemned to freedom." Knowing this in our hearts, we are filled with anxiety; we flee into the comfort of some predetermined role or some self-identical human nature. The task of an existential psychology thus becomes clear: it must be a singleminded unmasking of our inveterate self-delusion.[7]

This is the very stuff of existentialism. Drained of this iconoclastic fervor, this tragic vision, the term becomes empty and vapid. Yet these are the very themes which are most readily submerged as existentialism moves toward the side of humanistic psychology. The sense of novelty with which the writings of Ernest Becker were received in some quarters may be taken as a measure of how far this eviscerating tendency had progressed. For what Becker did was to reinterpret Freudian psychoanalysis, taking as his touchstone this sobering aspect of classical existentialism. A recognition of this face of existentialism is, in any case, the fulcral point for an understanding of our own typology. For the neglect of this aspect of existentialism cannot be dismissed as an accident of the humanistic temperament; it has rather to do with the humanist's precommitments, and with the commitments' logic. (1) The existentialist distrusts our self-presentation, whereas the humanist, reacting against the cynicism of Freud, inclines toward acceptance and affirmation. (2) The existentialist sees separation where the humanist, rejecting Freud's conflict theory, prefers images of reconciliation and wholeness. (3) The existentialist sees denial and flight where the humanist, in the face

---

[7] Jean-Paul Sartre, *Being and Nothingness: An Essay on Phenomenological Ontology*, trans. Hazel E. Barnes (New York: Philosophical Library, 1956), pp. 625ff.

of Freud's pessimism, posits a spontaneous penchant toward integration and growth. Clearly we have isolated within existentialism an aspect which is distinct from the phenomenological. We might call it the tragic vision; but since we have an eye toward method, let us speak of a "critical concern."

The two faces of existentialism, phenomenological and critical, may be taken as proof of the richness of this school. But to appreciate these aspects is also to admit the tension that exists between them. For (1) a relentless interrogation of our customary way of seeing ourselves is one method, a straightforward description of what presents itself is quite another. And (2) if we are convinced that humanity is wedded to denial and self-forgetfulness, we will be reluctant to treat experience in terms of manifest meaning as affirmed by the experiencing subject. Finally (3) an acute sense of separation and estrangement must surely tax the relational coherence of our being-in-the-world. In the face of these tensions one might even question whether there is such a thing as a unitary "existentialism." My own sense is that there can occur an interaction of concerns, a dialectical refinement, and that something of this sort has been at the core of classical existentialism. But for the present it is enough to observe that a dialectic cannot even begin to take hold until the concerns have been adequately recognized and distinguished.

A recognition of the critical concern has the further effect of surfacing a subterranean link between two unlikely partners, the existential psychologist and the orthodox psychoanalyst. The historian Gerald Izenberg has suggested that psychoanalysis and existentialism constitute two successive and related phases of this century's crisis of autonomy.[8] Erich Heller has remarked that Freudian psychoanalysis may be the most stringent attempt ever undertaken to interpret consciousness in a manner which is not tacitly hierarchical; and similarly Heidegger's invocation of *Dasein* may be seen as a thoroughgoing effort to elude certain hierarchical precommitments which attach to the term "human being."[9] Accordingly the affinities between existential psychology and Freudian psychoanalysis may be summarized by noting the following points of contrast to the humanistic alternative. (1) Both are bent upon unmasking our conventional self-presentation: the existentialist Nietzsche joins Freud and Marx within Ricoeur's "hermeneutic of suspicion."[10] And (2) both submit our lives to the sign of tragic separation: an analogue of the existentialist theme asserts itself among Freud interpreters as diverse as Otto Rank, Norman O. Brown and most recently

---

[8] Gerald N. Izenberg, *The Existentialist Critique of Freud: The Crisis of Autonomy* (Princeton: Princeton University Press, 1976).

[9] Erich Heller, "Observations on Psychoanalysis and Modern Literature," in *Psychiatry and the Humanities,* ed. Joseph H. Smith (New Haven: Yale University Press, 1976), 1.43; Walter Lowe, "On Using Heidegger," *Soundings* 60, no. 3 (Fall 1977): 264-84.

[10] Ricoeur, *Freud and Philosophy,* pp. 32-36.

Heinz Kohut.[11] Finally (3) as to denial and flight, Freud himself has singled out the concept of repression as the touchstone of psychoanalytic theory.[12] Thus the second bracket, which appears to the upper right of the diagram.

Finally, introducing the existentialist type serves to bring to light a tacit agreement between the avowed opponents, the humanistic psychologist and the Freudian psychoanalyst. Both lean toward positing some self-identical human nature, whether higher or lower, virtual or actual—and thus in the eyes of the existentialist, both tend to promote a subtle inauthenticity. Moreover, the existentialist critique of the alternatives at this point does not simply dissent on a point of description: in terms such as "bad faith" the moral passion is unmistakable. Yet for all its determination to set itself apart in substance and in tone, existentialism remains susceptible of certain alliances. It will adopt the rhetoric of humanism to convey a phenomenological disdain for the reductionism of the psychoanalyst, and it will acknowledge the Freudian unconscious as a canny though misguided premonition of the human penchant for self-forgetfulness. In sum, there is reason to recognize existentialism as a discrete alternative and yet to place it on a common footing alongside the other options.

This completes our lateral movement across the initial diagram. Before we proceed to the next section, however, we need one further refinement. To speak of a phenomenological concern must call to mind the philosophy of Edmund Husserl, "the father of phenomenology." This association is appropriate enough, for between Husserl and humanistic and existential psychology flow lines of strong historical influence. What is less commonly discussed, however, is the substantial discontinuity which obtains as well. Husserl's response to "the crisis of European man" was a spirited advocacy of a more rigorous philosophy. For the crisis sprang from a failure of nerve: our capacity for reflection, which is the ground of humanism, had never really entered into its own. It remained confused and self-forgetful, enmeshed in "the natural attitude," a naive immersion in the world; and for this irresolution the humanist must share the blame.[13] The diagnosis may sound existentialist, but the prescription which followed from it does not. For in Husserl's eyes a few phenomenological concerns and a prophetic posture do not a phenomenologist make: Husserl's solution looked not to engagement but to an intensified reflection. By a stringent discipline of

---

[11] Norman O. Brown, *Life Against Death: The Psychoanalytical Meaning of History* (New York: Random House, 1959), p. 115; Heinz Kohut, *The Restoration of the Self* (New York: International Universities Press, 1977), p. 91.

[12] Sigmund Freud, "An Autobiographical Study" in *The Standard Edition of the Complete Psychological Works of Sigmund Freud*, trans. under general editorship of James Strachey, 24 vols. (London: Hogarth Press, 1959), 20:30.

[13] Edmund Husserl, *Phenomenology and the Crisis of Philosophy: "Philosophy as Rigorous Science" and "Philosophy and the Crisis of European Man,"* trans. Quentin Lauer (New York: Harper and Row, 1965).

thought, self and world would eventually be seen to converge in the immanent self-transparency of "the transcendental ego."[14]

Even among those who presumed to understand this Husserlian vision, the majority chose to reject the project as the defiant boast of a moribund metaphysic. But skeptic and convert alike were agreed at least on this—that Husserl had succeeded in setting forth an acutely distinctive method. This is the awkward fact which gets obscured by the common, diffuse usage of the term "phenomenology." To keep Husserl's challenge before our minds, I wish therefore to distinguish from a broadly phenomenological "concern," the more rigorous phenomenological "method."[15] But as soon as we take that step, the itch for tidiness compels us to ask whether there should not be a further, complementary term, a "critical" method as well. I propose to argue that such is indeed the case, and for reasons which transcend the diagrammatic. Recent philosophy has evinced a mounting interest in the Frankfurt School of "critical theory," and within that movement the purest case is perhaps that of Theodor Adorno. Here as with Husserl we catch the visionary voice with its characteristic marks of intransigence and idiosyncracy; and with critical theory as with phenomenology, the reviews varied accordingly. We will have occasion to arrive at our own assessment in the course of the following section. For the present it is enough to add this last element to our schema, recognizing that it stands more as a question than as a datum.

II

Recognizing the overarching concerns, phenomenological and critical, helps us appreciate the psychological schools as something other than watertight compartments. The way in which the concerns overlap the schools shows how the positions may interpenetrate; it suggests that there is a logic to the way in which the schools have actually interacted. At the same time, however, the distinction which we have drawn between concern and method serves as a reminder that we are not simply dealing with an undisturbed spectrum. There are issues at stake, choices to be made, and it is to a clarification of these issues that the present section now turns. I propose to consider the entire schema—the two methods as well as the three schools—as an expanded five-part typology. We will examine these several options *seriatim*, seeking to understand the underlying logic by which they rise and fall.

[14] Edmund Husserl, *Ideas: General Introduction to Pure Phenomenology*, trans. W. R. Boyce Gibson (London: Allen and Unwin, 1931), pp. 232–34; Robert Sokolowski, *The Formation of Husserl's Concept of Constitution* (The Hague: Martinus Nijhoff, 1964), pp. 136–39.

[15] Cf. Herbert Spiegelberg, *The Phenomenological Movement: A Historical Introduction*, 2 vols. (The Hague: Martinus Nijhoff, 1960), 1:3ff.

1. Humanistic psychology

"Humanism" in psychology has become the rallying point for an amazing array of actual practices. Yet there is throughout the clan a certain family resemblance, among the salient features of which are an insistence upon holistic thinking and a championing of certain values.[16] Now much of the drama of humanistic psychology, and of psychology at large, is generated at just this point—by the dialectic of value and whole. To appreciate this dialectic we must first distinguish an initial, rather rhetorical level at which the two themes simply coalesce. The humanist frequently charges that both Freudianism and behaviorism have considered the person solely in terms of those lower aspects which are shared with the animal and material realms. What is needed is a more holistic psychology which has room for the higher aspects as well—namely those capacities or values which make us distinctively human. We are thus returned to the many-storied mansion. But beyond this initial point of hierarchical concord there lies a fundamental tension, which traces back to the psychology's ambivalence toward its very namesake, the humanism of the Enlightenment. For on the one hand, humanistic psychology stands in clear continuity with the Enlightenment; and in so doing it inherits a characteristically modern crisis in the relationship between notions of value and notions of the whole. On the other hand, humanistic psychology seeks to transcend the Enlightenment tradition; and in so doing it reaches toward a resolution, a renewed cooperation of value and whole.

To begin with the first aspect, we may recall that for the Enlightenment "the distinctively human" was a potent value term. In spelling out the concept, the Enlightenment tended to equate the distinctively human with the exercise of *freedom*. And then by an elision of thought it defined freedom as the ability to distinguish oneself—the ability to stand over against society, against the heteronomous "whole." This thrust toward individual liberation continues to exercise great appeal within humanistic psychology; it accounts for the side of humanistic psychology which opens in the direction of existentialism.

The second aspect of humanistic psychology stems rather from a rebellion against the Enlightenment, specifically a rebellion against a further definition of the distinctively human. For the Enlightenment also defined the distinctively human as the exercise of *reason*; and here once again the Enlightenment drifted from distinction to separation, tacitly honoring the notion of a disembodied mind. At this point the humanistic psychologist's rejection of the Enlightenment heritage is totally unambiguous: to be fully

---

[16] Anthony J. Sutich and Miles A. Vich, eds., *Readings in Humanistic Psychology* (New York: The Free Press, 1969), pp. 6–9; Orlo Strunk, "Humanistic Religious Psychology: A New Chapter in the Psychology of Religion," in *Current Perspectives in the Psychology of Religion*, ed. H. Newton Maloney (Grand Rapids: Eerdmans, 1977), p. 31.

human is to be in touch with our bodies, our affects are part of our very humanity. Nor is this a minor shift, as if one were simply adding another element to the picture. For the significance of affect is precisely that it puts us in touch with our larger context—in touch with the larger whole. Thus humanistic psychology has at least partially recognized that the problem with the tradition lies not so much in this or that definition, but in the persistent tendency in all its definitions to see distinctiveness as overagainst-ness, as if the specific were secured by isolation. It follows that when, in contrast, the humanistic psychologist makes central to our humanity the capacity for openness, encounter or love, the intent is more than sentimental; it is an effort to appreciate the distinctive precisely in that which is most relational. Thus this side of humanistic psychology asserts what the individualism of the Enlightenment would deny: that the distinctive is best affirmed by its being grounded within a larger whole. Accordingly this is the "transpersonal" side of humanistic psychology, which faces in the direction of a comprehensive metaphysic.[17]

The search for a larger context, like the interest in Eastern religions which often accompanies it, may be profound or superficial. A good litmus is the degree to which the humanist recognizes that in contemporary culture an appeal to values raises as many questions as it resolves. It is not enough to affirm the human quest for meaning; one must face the unnerving question of whether meaning is found within the world or simply projected upon it. Similarly one must ask of values, are they subjective or objective, human craft or a gift of the cosmos? In effect it is a matter of recognizing the crisis of which we spoke earlier, the crisis in the relationship of value and whole. Paul Ricoeur has acknowledged that ". . . philosophy at the present time is entirely at an impasse concerning the problem of the origin of values. We are condemned to vacillate between an impossible creation of values and an impossible intuition of values. This theoretical failure is reflected in the practical antinomy between submission and rebellion that infects the daily concerns of education, politics and ethics."[18] It would be unfair to stick the psychologist with these questions, for they are not of the psychologist's making. But the psychologist must be asked to join others in confronting the common quandary. For in certain cases one senses in the advocate of values that heady and unreflective buoyancy which is the mark of the recent convert.

In other cases, however, it is clear that a response to the crisis has been embodied in the very notion of a humanistic psychology. It is an effort to

---

[17] Strunk, "Humanistic Religious Psychology," p. 34; Robert E. Ornstein, ed., *The Nature of Human Consciousness: A Book of Readings* (San Francisco: W. H. Freeman and Co., 1968). For an illuminating semipopular discussion of issues raised by transpersonal psychology, see Philip Slater, *The Wayward Gate: Science and the Supernatural* (Boston: Beacon Press, 1977).

[18] Ricoeur, *Conflict of Interpretations*, p. 449.

fuse the inwardness of the humanistic tradition with the objectivity of empirical science; it is in this fashion that humanistic psychology essays the inescapable task of thinking at one and the same time in terms of the distinctive and in terms of the whole. The boundary stance joining science and humanism commends itself for reasons which are both symbolic and practical. Symbolically, to live on the boundary, at the point of greatest tension, is a way of bearing witness to a more fundamental ground which transcends our notions of subjectivity and objectivity. And practically the boundary stance represents a straightforward decision to get on with answering the needs at hand—extending to science the virtues of the heart, bringing to sentiment the rigor of the mind and offering to all who seek it the powers of a healing empathy.

2. Phenomenological method

From another angle however a mixed method is no method, but confusion; and a boundary stance will just reinforce the cacophany of the present crisis. For the phenomenologist the source of the confusion is the failure to see that the distinctively human is precisely not what the humanist makes of it, a part within a larger whole. Rather our distinctiveness is to be found in our capacity to *have* a whole—which is to say, in our capacity to "intend" a world. Indeed one might almost say that the revolution of phenomenology is to have placed the seeming whole, the world, within the distinctively human. It is here that the paths divide. For the humanistic psychologist can acknowledge the point and yet see the issue as a relative question. Between subjective and objective, "inner" and "outer," which is the part and which the whole? Why neither and both: the mistake is in thinking one has to choose. The human paradox is the deeper truth, that both perspectives are true. For the phenomenologist, in contrast, the choice cannot possibly be resolved into complementary viewpoints. The issue is rather a demand for a radical conversion of the mind, another level of reflection. To Husserl the naturalism of the scientistic worldview was idolatry, and his response was properly prophetic. For to bargain with idols is impossible; it is to place oneself in a position which is already fatally compromised.[19]

The results of the Husserlian rigor may be illustrated with regard to being-in-the-world, the leitmotif of the "phenomenological concern." Humanist and phenomenologist are at one in affirming the phrase, but to the humanist "being-in-the-world" means that we participate *in* the world— whereas for the phenomenologist it means that we participate *in the process of intending* a world. It is in this way that phenomenology opens up a second level of reflection. It steps back to ask the antecedent question, "why is there something rather than nothing at all?" It shakes the dogmatic slumbers of

---

[19] Husserl, *Phenomenology and the Crisis of Philosophy.*

the "natural attitude," which naively assumes the givenness of the world
and then fancies itself scientific because it proceeds to inquire within it.
Moreover the question is not simply a matter of propadeutic, which could
be addressed and then set aside. For the phenomenologist responds to the
question by laying bare the process of intending; and that process, once
understood, radically alters our apprehension of every experience. Each
thing, each experience without exception, will be seen as a "presentation":
that is, as the meaningful "noematic" face of a "noetic," meaning-giving
act.[20]

It is in this fashion that phenomenology proposes to be critical. It is
bent upon following through the Copernican revolution of viewpoint initiated by Immanuel Kant—namely the recognition of *the all-pervasive and
generative activity of the knowing subject.* The extent of the revolution may be
gauged by the impact it has upon our common, pre-critical notions of
wholeness and value. The world which once seemed the whole is subjectiv-
ized, becoming a function of intentional activity. And values are not simply
invoked and presupposed; their very constitution becomes the topic of
methodical scrutiny. Yet the critical shift is not simply negative: Kant's aim
was to "justify" such conceptions as space, time, freedom, and God, which
had been merely speculative. Similarly the aim of Husserl's noetic-noematic
setting is to stabilize the conceptual staggering to which Ricoeur refers in
his comment on values. Indeed it can be said that we understand Husserl in
the measure that we come to appreciate the critical and the foundational
aspects of phenomenology not as mutually exclusive, nor even as complementary moments—but as internally related: the two faces of a single
quest.[21]

Further testimony to the positive character of phenomenology's critical
commitment is the fact that in the very process whereby the contents of our
everyday world and everyday values are subjected to scrutiny, the essential
human activities of forming gestalts and valuing reassert themselves in
another guise. The comprehensive noetic-noematic field becomes the new
whole; indeed it arranges itself in strata which point in the direction of
hierarchy. And while the mission of the phenomenologist is not to direct
but to describe, that firm descriptive intent has the effect of exalting lucidity to the level of a presiding norm. Now these affirmations become the
target, in turn, for the existentialist's critique of phenomenology. There is
between phenomenologist and existentialist a kinship which was implied by
our diagram and which is confirmed by the recent critique of the everyday
in terms of certain founding acts; for in existentialist terms such acts are the

---

[20] Husserl, *Ideas*, pp. 255ff.
[21] Pierre Thévenaz, *What is Phenomenology? and Other Essays*, ed. James M. Edie, trans. James
M. Edie, Charles Courtney, and Paul Brockelman (Chicago: Quadrangle Books, 1962), pp.
93ff.

root of our fundamental responsibility. But the existentialist senses in phenomenology a certain lofty self-possession, a feigned transcendence of the human condition of limitation and mortality. In the eyes of the existentialist, phenomenology betrays its own intent of being straightforwardly descriptive—for in Husserl's realm of meaning there is no place for life's elemental absurdity.[22]

Thus once again the conceptual path divides and again each way is honorable. To the phenomenologist, negative meaning is meaning still—else we could not talk about it. The phenomenologist may well respond to the existentialist that the community of discourse has suffered long enough from the voices of haste and alarm. In time of crisis the true existential courage, perhaps, is not to spread despair but to stand by the task, the nurturance of meaning, which Being has bequeathed us.

3. Existential psychology

But for the existentialist the notion of a transcendental ego, however chastened, can only encourage us in our hankering for the chimerical vision of a superhuman self-identity. Much as the phenomenologist criticized the humanist for failing to follow through on Kant's Copernican revolution, so the existentialist chides the phenomenologist. For phenomenology affirms the Kantian insight that the experiencing subject is pervasively active—and yet phenomenology may be charged with retaining from the earlier empiricism a quasi-perceptualist model of truth, in the notions of "intuition" and "fulfillment"; and it may be argued that contra Kant this finally locates truth not in act, but in static identity.[23] In this light the key existentialist concepts are aimed at guaranteeing what the phenomenologist let slip, the centrality of human activity; and this means that despite appearances, the concepts are not simply negative. This is true of even so extreme a case as the existentialist's preoccupation with death. Had we an eternity in which to act, our time would have little meaning. Because we do not, time matters. But this is to say that our lives can have meaning not simply in spite of, but because of, the constant fact of mortality.

The charge against phenomenology, in brief, is that it is insufficiently critical. Phenomenology affirms Kant's effort to gain critical distance, to

---

[22] Sartre, *Being and Nothingness*, pp. 438–39.

[23] This criticism represents a disputed point in the interpretation of phenomenology; useful in this regard is the study by Alphonse de Waelhens, *Phénoménologie et vérité: Essai sur l'évolution de l'idée de vérité chez Husserl et Heidegger* (Paris: Presses Universitaires, 1953). The critique of identity theory has been formative for the thought of the Frankfurt School. See Theodor W. Adorno, *Negative Dialectics*, trans. E. B. Ashton (New York: Seabury Press, 1973), pp. 3–35 *et passim*; Jürgen Habermas, *Knowledge and Human Interests*, trans., Jeremy J. Shapiro (Boston: Beacon Press, 1971), pp. 5, 301ff.; Martin Jay, *The Dialectical Imagination: A History of the Frankfurt School and the Institute of Social Research, 1923-1950* (Boston: Little, Brown and Co., 1973), pp. 46–47.

fight free of the immediacies of the natural attitude, and yet at the same time it unreflectively perpetuates an ideal of truth as presence: intuitive and immediate.[24]

Now if this is indeed the import of the existentialist's dissent, it follows that the further step which existentialism proposes is a step *within* the transcendental context. This point must be stressed in the face of the popular identification of existentialism with humanistic psychology, as if the existentialist dissent represented a common sense dismissal of Husserlian "idealism," a simple rejection of transcendental thought. This misapprehension is partly the work of the existentialist's own rhetoric; like the language of drama which it resembles, it seems to disdain reflection in favor of intuitive recognition. But I wish to suggest that, apart from the progression of argument which we have been tracing, existentialism loses its conceptual girding, resolves to pure emotion and drifts toward empty self-parody.

A case in point is the central issue of one's relationship to oneself. For the existentialist this self-self relationship comes close to being the determinative whole; certainly in any case a shouldering of the relationship is the existentialist's determinative value. Kierkegaard set the stage with the first page of *The Sickness Unto Death* by contending that "the self is a relation which relates itself to its own self. . . ." But in the pragmatic atmosphere of humanistic psychology, this vision becomes oddly distended. To ask how one feels about one's self-image is not yet to engage a more radical self-self relationship. And to advocate holism is to miss the insight that the self is not simply a whole, but a whole-whole relationship. This paradoxical relationship is a distinctively modern notion, one which Kant made possible and Hegel made essential.[25] When Sartre berates the experimentalist and the psychoanalyst for trying to construct out of parts the whole-whole relationship which they already, uncritically, must presuppose, his criticism is simply an adaptation of the peculiar holism of Kant's transcendental epistemology. When Sartre holds that the failure is moral, a ruse of bad faith, he is recalling the "unhappy consciousness" as Hegel once evoked it.[26] Sartre, for his part, was mindful of this rootage. Subsequent events seem to confirm that, severed from this context, the existentialist argument drifts toward the one-dimensional.

Accordingly, the critics of existentialism, to turn to them, must be distinguished as to whether or not they engage the issue within the transcendental context. It is commonly acknowledged for example that existentialism

---

[24] Martin Heidegger, *Being and Time*, trans. John Macquarrie and Edward Robinson (New York: Harper and Brothers, 1962), p. 47; Sokolowski, *Formation of Husserl's Concept of Constitution*, pp. 200–201.

[25] Cf. Lionel Trilling, *Sincerity and Authenticity* (Cambridge, MA: Harvard University Press, 1971), pp. 26ff.

[26] Richard Bernstein, *Praxis and Action: Contemporary Philosophies of Human Activity* (Philadelphia: University of Pennsylvania Press, 1971), pp. 84ff.

has little room for the insights of sociology. But stated so abruptly, the remark suggests a farrago of the two approaches, transcendental and empirical—without a commensurate awareness of the conceptual anomalies which such a mixed method must entail. The more promising tack is once again to draw upon warrants which are common to transcendental discourse, to suggest respects in which existentialism too is insufficiently critical. Husserl's uncovering of intentional activity was critical in a sense derived broadly from Kant: it displayed the conditions of the possibility of the natural attitude. The existentialist's treatment of Husserl, in turn, with regard to immediacy and mediation, shows remarkable resemblance to Hegel's critique of Kant.[27] An imminent scrutiny of existentialism will present itself as a further extension of this classic debate.

As background to the critique of existentialism, we may recall that existentialism concurs with phenomenology on the centrality of the self-self relationship. The existentialist turn upon phenomenology is simply to add that, *de facto,* the relationship is never fully realized, it can never resolve to a condition of self-identity. Rather we find that we are sundered within by our "thrownness" and temporality; and it is only in recognizing this comfortless reality that we attain to a condition of authenticity. At just this point, however, the critic of existentialism may charge that the existentialist has in fact capitulated to a subtle variant of the old dream of self-identity. For in acknowledging *that* my condition is one of relentless separation, I enter upon an undeluded correspondence *with* my condition, which is the very meaning of authenticity. And can this be anything other than the correspondence theory of truth, once rejected and now reborn as a self-identity of the *will?* The question is an adaptation of Hegel's critique of romantic consciousness; and the aim is Hegel's aim, to preserve in performance, and not just in word, the Kantian insight into the subject's all-pervasive activity. It is well and good for the existentialist to have dramatized the crisis precipitated by historicity and temporality. But when it comes to the existentialist's response to that crisis, one must ask whether the subject's act can remain actual once it has been so compacted within a timeless "moment" of decision.

The immanent critique of existentialism is represented by the Frankfurt School of critical theory; again the ways divide and there is honorable disagreement. The point at issue approaches being a theological disagreement

---

[27] In concentrating upon the theme of mediation, I am reading the whole of Hegel in light of one aspect of his thought, the aspect stressed particularly by Herbert Marcuse, *Reason and Revolution: Hegel and the Rise of Social Theory* (New York: Oxford University Press, 1941). Equally important to any comprehensive assessment of Hegel is the more familiar aspect which is allied with "the philosophy of identity." Habermas examines the interplay of both aspects in his opening chapter, "Hegel's Critique of Kant: Radicalization or Abolition of the Theory of Knowledge." A similar interplay provides the dynamic of much of the present essay.

over the locus of original sin. For the existentialist, all creativity traces back to the individual: to say that a group "acts" is to speak in a way which is extended at best, and finally misleading. For our root temptation is the anonymous herd, a forgetfulness of the individual among the pretensions of the collectivity. And our tragic grandeur is our ability to refuse a mute immortality which is not more, but less, than human.

4. Critical theory

While existentialism sides with Kierkegaard on the character of original sin, the critical theorist favors Marx. The great temptation is that of the bourgeois individualist, to cover over the harsh realities of our concrete social condition. But it must be stressed that critical theory is not a mixed method in the vein of conventional "dialectical materialism," the forced marriage of an idealist logic and the data of economics. Rather critical theory emerges out of the transcendental sphere, by arguments generated within that sphere; and the issues at stake are those with which we have already become familiar.

This placing of critical theory is confirmed by a number of recent commentators. Susan Buck-Morss selects phenomenology and existentialism as key points of reference; and once again the cardinal issue is mediation: "where Adorno felt existentialism (as well as phenomenology and *Lebensphilosophie*) made its mistake was in accepting 'natural' phenomena as 'given' immediately in experience. Hegel had already demonstrated the illusory nature of such attempts at 'concreteness' in the opening pages of *The Phenomenology of Mind.* . . ."[28] Moreover, just as Husserl saw in "the natural attitude" a certain idolatry and just as the existentialist saw in the transcendental ego a suprahuman presumption, so the critical theorist too has a moral stake in the debate. For regarded in the false isolation of immediacy, the object becomes an "enchantment," a "fetish" and a "fate."[29] In effect, the error of previous thinkers lay in short-circuiting the critical arc: "by stopping with the immediately given object, they did not see past this fetish-like appearance, whose reified form Lukács had analyzed as 'second nature.'"[30]

This concept of "second nature," which derives from Hegel, is altogether crucial. An example would be certain class differences: they are forms of domination which have wrapped themselves in a cloak of inevitability, as if they were somehow rooted in nature. Yet they are not nature

---

[28] Susan Buck-Morss, *The Origin of Negative Dialectics: Theodor W. Adorno, Walter Benjamin and the Frankfurt Institute* (New York: The Free Press, 1977), p. 73. For an argument which in many respects parallels that of the present essay, see Garbis Kortian, *Metacritique: The Philosophical Argument of Jürgen Habermas*, trans. John Raffan (Cambridge: Cambridge University Press, 1980).

[29] Buck-Morss, *Origin of Negative Dialectics*, p. 55.

[30] Ibid., p. 73.

but the congealed, sedimented results of past historical acts, they are "second nature." To expose the oppression which hides behind such mystification is the chief task of the critical theorist. Thus critical theory does not propose a mixed method which would seek to supplement the individualism of existentialism with certain empirical observations drawn from another field such as sociology. Indeed there is an important sense in which critical theory seeks not to offset, but to radicalize the existentialist's own distinctive insight. For like the existentialist, the critical theorist is bent upon uncovering our human freedom and responsibility; and in the one case as in the other, the exposure is profoundly unsettling. The difference is simply that more often than the existentialist, the critical theorist finds the evidences of that alienated freedom by an analytical penetration *into* the givens of the social order, rather than by standing over against them.

A companion piece to the issue of mediation throughout our investigations has been the question of truth, and specifically the critique of the correspondence theory of truth with its telos of identity. Here too critical theory may be seen as continuing the earlier argument; thus Max Horkheimer, who along with Adorno originated the earlier critical theory, took it as his task to describe "the death of the identity principle upon which bourgeois metaphysics had been founded. . . ."[31] But the target was not simply classical metaphysics; the critical theorists so formulated the attack upon identity as to include a criticism of the concept of intentionality, which was so central to phenomenology. Moreover Adorno, for his part, was not content to reject intentionality. He undertook the further step of expounding an alternative doctrine of "*un*intentional truth," a doctrine of truth as *non*-identity. This remarkable proposal may be understood as an insistence that historical circumstances arise inadvertently, behind our backs, and even ironically, contrary to our intentions. But the decisive thing about the notion of unintentional truth was that it eventuated in the endorsement of a form of materialism—in critical theory the rejection of intentionality "converged with materialism in its claim that the object was the source of truth."[32]

Thus we have succeeded in locating critical theory at the confluence of the transcendental, phenomenological tradition and a certain form of materialism. But everything depends on how these terms and their relationship are understood. Buck-Morss suggests that the theorists' new direction "was 'materialist' not so much in the Marxian sense as in the simpler sense of pre-Kantian empiricism."[33] This gloss is useful as a reminder that the theorists' appropriation of Marx was not doctrinaire and as a measure of the theorists' determination to gain a point of leverage outside of the transcendental sphere. But Buck-Morss's reading runs counter to her own recognition that the

[31] Ibid., p. 70.
[32] Ibid., p. 78.
[33] Ibid.

theorists criticized Husserl and others for their characteristically pre-Kantian practice of selecting for reflection objects drawn from the natural order, such as trees, rather than objects which more clearly bore the social imprint.[34] This criticism on the part of the critical theorists is evidence that we may say of them, as we said of the existentialists, that even in adopting those postures which appear most antithetical to transcendental discourse, they were prompted by concerns derived from that very tradition.

The prime concern is of course the Hegelian issue of mediation. But the transcendental rootage goes deeper than this formal concern: the theorists press Hegel's issue for precisely Hegel's reasons—namely defending and extending the Kantian insight into the subject's pervasive, generative activity. For as we saw in examining the concept of second nature, a determination to penetrate to our underlying activity and responsibility is at the heart of the critical enterprise. In its refusal of transcendental pretensions for transcendental reasons, by way of a non-transcendental perspective—inserting materialism into the reflective arc in order to avert a premature cloture—critical theory represents a sort of eschatological postponement of all transcendental completion. Thus the critical theorists arrive at a profoundly dialectical stance toward the transcendental tradition. On the strength of this dialectical stance we may conclude that critical theory does embody an integral method, quite distinct from the broader matter of "critical concern."

Turning finally to evaluation, we may recall one further theme of our inquiry, namely the uneasy relationship which we have observed between notions of value and notions of the whole. Critical theory is an unmasking of the false values generated by ideology, which is the self-inflation of special interests to the level of an oppressive metaphysic, a spurious whole. This is the sense of Adorno's much-quoted maxim, "the whole is the false."[35] At the same time the critical theorists drew heavily upon a tacit recognition of a more authentic, more concrete whole; they agreed with Lukács that "the objects of the empirical world are to be understood as objects of a totality, i.e., as the aspects of a total situation caught up in the process of historical change."[36] Yet this latter whole could never be brought to articulation. Despite its concreteness, or rather precisely because it was so radically concrete, this social totality assumed the elusive but determinative station of a regulative idea. A similar situation obtained as regards the theorists' implicit anthropology and their implicit values; Martin Jay has observed, "Dialectics was superb at attacking other systems' pretensions to truth, but when it came to articulating the grounds of its own assumptions

---

[34] Ibid., p. 73.

[35] Theodor W. Adorno, *Minima Moralia: Reflections from Damaged Life,* trans. E. F. N. Jephcott (London: New Left Books, 1974), p. 50.

[36] George Lukács, *History and Class Consciousness: Studies in Marxist Dialectics,* trans. Rodney Livingstone (Cambridge, MA: MIT Press, 1971), p. 162. Cf. Martin Jay, "The Concept of Totality," *Telos,* no. 30 (Summer 1977): 117–37.

and values, it fared less well. Like its implicit reliance on a negative anthropology, 'critical theory' had a basically insubstantial concept of reason and truth, rooted in social conditions and yet outside of them, connected with *praxis* yet keeping its distance from it."[37]

Critical theory is not a rounded theory so much as it is a tactic—a sort of interim ethic, a way of waiting without idols in a time of eschatological postponement. But there is no concealing the fact that this strategic incompleteness, however appropriate, does foster certain ironic dependencies.[38] We find ourselves returned by the requirements of the critics themselves to the humanists' original insistence upon some judicious articulation of the distinctively human, of the attendant values and of the embracing whole.

5. Freudian psychoanalysis

Whatever their differences, phenomenology, existentialism and critical theory agree on certain premises drawn from Kant's critique of the natural attitude. When juxtaposed to this transcendental accord, the headstrong materialism of Freudian psychoanalysis must seem a misplaced item, a discordant note. But the present essay has contended that, nevertheless, the transcendental background may be the missing link we have needed in order to clarify certain issues in psychoanalysis and in its relationship to humanistic psychology. To make this case now I must do more than simply show that between psychoanalysis and the transcendental discussion there exist certain external similarities. I will have to demonstrate that the similarities may be used to illumine psychoanalysis in its own right.

The grounds for my argument have been prepared by Paul Ricoeur in his painstaking study of Freud. Ricoeur has shown that Freud's thought is never simply that of a positivist; it is simultaneously a hermeneutic, an act of cultural interpretation. Freud speaks not only a "force language" of drives and impulses, but also a "meaning language" of dreams and wishes, of purposes and texts.[39] Philip Rieff mounts a similar argument in a book which is aptly titled *Freud: The Mind of the Moralist*. Rieff holds that contrary to the common image of him, Freud actually rejected the materialist position according to which "mind is the agent of the body"; in its place he introduced the pregnant insight that "the body exists as a symptom of mental demands."[40] This crucial turn away from naturalism is central to Rieff's conception of Freud as moralist, as it is to Ricoeur's conception of psychoanalysis as hermeneutic. We need only add that the turn is equally central to Freud's affinity with the Kantian

---

[37] Jay, *The Dialectical Imagination*, p. 63.

[38] Buck-Morss, *Origin of Negative Dialectics*, p. 190.

[39] Ricoeur, *Freud and Philosophy*, pp. 65-67.

[40] Philip Rieff, *Freud: The Mind of the Moralist* (Garden City, NJ: Doubleday, 1959), p. 6; Don S. Browning, *Generative Man: Psychoanalytic Perspectives* (Philadelphia: Westminster Press, 1973), pp. 42-43.

revolution. In both cases our conventional paradigms are shaken by the discovery of an underlying decision, an originary act.

Now it is at just this point that the analyses of Freud by theologians and humanists commonly stop short—as if the Kantian turn were itself an answer, and not a whole new set of questions as well. It is often shown that Freud is not simply a materialist, that he presupposes a certain freedom, a certain transcendence. And it is often shown that he has affinities with the transcendental turn, particularly by way of a convergence between psychoanalysis and existentialism. In this manner affirmations of three distinct sorts intermingle as if they were identical, or as if they were mutually reinforcing. To stick with the example of freedom: freedom is affirmed as a certain *transcendence*, as a crucial *value* and as a consequence of the transcendental turn toward the subject. Conflations of this sort are the substructure of many discussions of psychoanalysis and humanistic psychology—regardless of whether the discussion then concludes by locating the conflation solely on the side of humanistic psychology, thus favoring that position, or by placing the conflation between the two positions as a ground for common agreement.

But the burden of our entire argument has been that the very attractiveness of this bundle of affirmations serves to disguise certain fundamental dilemmas, and that the seriousness of these dilemmas is dramatized by the restless interchange, the mutual critique and complementarity, which we observe among several schools of modern thought. Thus it is no solution to conflate transcendence with the transcendental: the Kantian turn is nothing if not a sustained critique of the metaphysical transcendence which is one component of humanistic psychology. And similarly the dialectic of value and whole which we have traced throughout the transcendental sphere bears witness that the impact of Kant upon the affirmation of values is as unsettling as it is suggestive.

Such are the lessons of our discussion thus far. Now the task is to show how the same issues reassert themselves when we take up psychoanalysis in its own right. Let us consider the way in which a simple shift of emphasis in our reading of psychoanalysis may precipitate certain sharp and unattended changes. On the one hand you can stress the fact *that* there is an underlying human act. Reality takes on a more human face; the awareness of mental sources will give you a *psycho*analysis analogous to phenomenology, with an opening toward humanistic psychology. There will be a cordial relationship of mutual reinforcement between your sense of value and your sense of the whole; and correspondingly, a supportive accord between individual and society. Rieff is speaking in this vein when he says that Freud "restored an ethical, and therefore a social, conception of human sickness";[41] and many have been the voices contending that this aspect of matters is the final truth about psychoanalysis.

---

[41] Rieff, *Mind of the Moralist*, p. 12.

On the other hand you may stress that while there is such an act, it remains elusive and self-forgetful. It was this shift which caused the Kantian turn to reveal its other aspect, that of a radical decentering of the self: and similarly psychoanalysis, on the premise that our innermost acts escape immediate introspection, will press upon us a variety of techniques by which the elusive activity may be unearthed and secured. The techniques will be those of a psychoanalysis which is bent upon the dissolution of those heteronomous values and those peremptory wholes which inhibit the free exercise of autonomy. Therapy will still be moral in the sense of having a human telos, but the telos is now reduced to a negative freedom, a "freedom from"; and a freedom of this sort corrodes the loyalties which knit together the society and the individual. This is the unsettling logic which led Rieff from Freud the moralist to *The Triumph of the Therapeutic*. For our part we need only note that Rieff's "therapeutic personality" is the direct descendant of the existentialist. There is just one difference, which tellingly reflects that which is specific to this aspect of psychoanalysis. For the therapeutic personality, in contrast to the existentialist, even the ultimate questions have been subjected to the implacable analysis. Ultimate concern has come to seem a hang-up.

Just as Rieff's initial turn toward seeing Freud as moralist parallels the Kantian turn toward an awareness of the subject's all-pervasive activity, so the subsequent shift of emphasis in the direction of analytic suspicion parallels the Hegelian move toward critical mediation. Now I have argued that central to Hegel's project is a determination to secure the Kantian insight; and indeed all of Hegel's philosophy may be read as a long but deliberate detour designed to accomplish this end. In like fashion we may say that one would never go to the trouble of refining the mediating techniques of analytic suspicion if one were not persuaded that there is an underlying act to be got at. Nor is it only with regard to its aims and presuppositions that psychoanalysis affirms the subject's activity: Jürgen Habermas has shown on similarly Hegelian grounds that the very method by which analysis aims to increase the subject's autonomy is, itself, a self-correcting intersubjective activity.[42] This I take to be at least part of the significance of speaking of analysis as "praxis."

But psychoanalysis is praxis of a most peculiar sort; and it is at this point, in treating the distinctiveness of psychoanalysis, that Habermas proves least helpful. I propose therefore to turn instead to an interpretation of Ricoeur's exposition of Freud's distinctive "language of force."[43] The entirety of *Freud and Philosophy* grows from the premise that Freud's mixed discourse of force

---

[42] Habermas, *Knowledge and Human Interests*, pp. 214ff.

[43] In a more recent treatment of Freud, Ricoeur would seem to have confirmed this line of interpretation; see Ricoeur, "The Question of Proof in Freud's Psychoanalytic Writings," in *The Philosophy of Paul Ricoeur: An Anthology of His work*, ed. Charles E. Reagan and David Stewart (Boston: Beacon Press, 1978).

language and meaning language is not an idiosyncracy or a muddle, but the very "raison d'être of psychoanalysis." In chapter 1 we saw that a central argument for this irreducibility of the mixed discourse is the manner in which that discourse reflects a crucial peculiarity of the analytic praxis. For while the analytic session is indeed an interpersonal encounter, what is distinctive about it is that in this case the interpersonal relationship itself is treated as a *technique*. One might almost conclude that the innovation of psychoanalysis is to have made of the I-Thou encounter the object, and even the means, of a certain manipulation. This is the difficult reality which is transcribed in Freud's language of force. Ricoeur says that this objectifying language portrays the person insofar as she or he "has been and remains a Thing"; we have sharpened Ricoeur's point by saying that the language portrays persons insofar as their intersubjective relationships may be properly *treated as* things. For the analytic session focusses upon "resistance, transference, repetition"; this vocabulary and this sequence are at the core of the therapeutic situation.

Thus we find that Freud's mixed discourse points to a position within psychoanalysis which closely parallels the peculiar materialism of the Frankfurt School;[44] and with this final step we may have sufficient evidence for the pertinence of the transcendental background to an understanding of psychoanalysis. It must be stressed, however, that we have been dealing in parallels and analogies. Despite these approximations to the transcendental, there is a side of Freud's materialism which remains resolutely pre-Kantian. One may perhaps regret this, but regret is no warrant for allowing the flatfooted reality of what Freud actually said to evanesce into the hermeneutical subtleties of what one feels he should have meant. Freudian psychoanalysis finds it proper setting outside the transcendental sphere—but in the most intimate proximity to it.

To the degree that we have now succeeded in showing that the transcendental background does illumine psychoanalysis, the illumination may be attributed to the fact that psychoanalysis had already been attempting, in effect, to replicate several of the philosophic options within itself, on the basis of its own premises. Earlier we saw that humanistic psychology tries in a similar fashion to fuse the transcendental and the scientific-empirical, and that existentialism is shaped by its effort to hold together the phenomenological and the critical. In effect we may say that each option seeks to incorporate the

---

[44] The argument may be further extended by reference to a number of themes from critical theory. Martin Jay remarks, "the revisionists' vaunted sociological 'correction' of Freud really amounted to little more than the smoothing over of social contradictions. By removing the biological roots of psychoanalysis, they had transformed it into a kind of *Geisteswissenschaft* and a means of social hygiene. Their desexualization was part of a denial of the conflict between essence and appearance, of the chasm between true gratification and the pseudo-happiness of contemporary civilization" (Jay, *Dialectical Imagination*, p. 104). Cf. Herbert Marcuse, *Eros and Civilization: A Philosophical Inquiry into Freud* (Boston: Beacon Press, 1955); Jay, *Dialectical Imagination*, pp. 106–12.

strengths of the other options, on the basis of its own premises. This suggests in turn that the sequence of options which we have traversed might best be conceived neither as a series of watertight compartments nor as an intermingling spectrum, but as a complex pattern of monads, each reflecting within itself a distinctive effort to grasp the entirety.

III

Much of this essay may be summarized by reference to the original diagram. At the center sits existential psychology, a microcosm of the larger philosophic tensions. Moving out a step in each direction, we might trace a circle which would describe the realm of transcendental discourse: the study has argued that phenomenology, existentialism and critical theory must be understood in terms of their common Kantian rootage; even their differences reflect a broadly Hegelian effort to preserve the essential Kantian insight, the transcendental turn. Yet another step and we encounter the positions which many earlier discussions had taught us to assume as antithetical. We can now appreciate the extent to which Freudian psychoanalysis and humanistic psychology in fact amount to mirror images of one another: the mixed method of humanistic psychology and the mixed discourse of Freudian psychoanalysis represent comparable efforts to fuse the Kantian discovery of subjectivity with various understandings of the requirements of the natural sciences. Thus both might be located on the boundary of the transcendental realm; but if we allow the philosophers to define the transcendental turn as an all-or-nothing conversion, we must reckon that the positions lie outside that realm, though in the greatest proximity to it. A last step and we arrive at two positions which, because of their distinctively metaphysical character, are properly placed at the furthest remove from the transcendental core. Finally there is in addition to this horizontal movement a vertical tension between the clinical praxis of the humanistic, existential and Freudian therapies and the more disengaged theorizing of the phenomenologist and the critical theorist—a tension which is mediated but not resolved by the sharing of certain phenomenological and critical concerns.

Now typologies of this sort are useful in anticipating the strengths and liabilities of various alternatives. By the same token, however, the schematic viewpoint makes it difficult to come to even a provisional decision favoring one position over against another. Existentialism may seem the most central option, but then phenomenology may be more rigorous and critical theory more self-aware; humanistic psychology is perhaps more comprehensive but Freudian psychoanalysis may be more realistic. . . . Each position has its virtues, but there is always another side as well. In this manner the possessor of the master schema may drift into a bemused contemplation which is faintly complacent, a posture which is self-forgetful in its very sophistication. To extricate ourselves from this lifeless equipose, I think it imperative that we keep in touch with the thrust of our investigations. Time and again we observed that, in actual practice, what tends to get pushed aside is not just any random aspect of matters, but one particular facet—that which we may now call in a comprehensive way the "critical." Indeed a convenient way of making this crucial point is simply to recall the several uses which have been made of this protean term. First the term was employed in the manner of common usage; and it was noted, following Tillich and Niebuhr, that a certain critical edge is often lost in the course of revising Freud. Secondly the term was used in the stricter sense of Kant's "critical philosophy," and it was proposed that the transcendental discussion which Kant initiated may be the neglected element in many discussions of psychology. Thirdly the term was used to represent the Hegelian insistence upon the necessity of mediation, and it was argued that this is a requirement which even Kant himself did not fully appreciate. Finally the term was used in the manner of the Frankfurt School of critical theory, and we found reason to take seriously the contention that such analysis strikes upon entrenched resistances, resistances which are not only individual but institutional as well.

A similar muting of the critical aspect may be discerned in even so able a commentator as Paul Ricoeur. The achievement of *Freud and Philosophy* lies not only in its close study of the Freudian texts, but also in its refusal to follow the lead of many earlier studies in simply adjusting psychoanalysis in the direction of phenomenology. What is bracing about Ricoeur is the robust affirmation that the distinctively critical aspect of psychoanalysis has positive value in its own right. Earlier I suggested that in its actual execution Ricoeur's work falls short of this intent. It is now possible to propose that the slippage may stem in part from his decision to view Freud under the rubric of a "hermeneutic of suspicion." The decision is consonant with Ricoeur's concern for philosophy of language, but I believe there are important respects in which the category "hermeneutic" proves insufficiently comprehensive, so that it skews the case which Ricoeur aims to make. For Ricoeur understands hermeneutics to be deeply allied with phenomenology: and one must wonder whether, by virtue of this alliance, the very notion of a "*hermeneutic* of suspicion" does not so tip the balance of discussion as to blunt from the outset the suspicion's critical edge.

For this reason I believe that the transcendental setting of the question is finally the more comprehensive: it better enables us to appreciate the origins and interactions of both aspects, the phenomenological *and* the critical. When viewed strictly within the context of hermeneutics, the birth of radical suspicion tends to seem an anomaly, a mutation of modern culture suggesting something of the paranoid or the perverse. The transcendental background, in contrast, reveals the critical as arising out of the internal requirements of phenomenology, as an effort to safeguard the formative insight upon which phenomenology itself is grounded. This is by no means to detract from the very real value of hermeneutical discussion, over against the earlier, more flatly metaphysical point of view. But it is to suggest that the importance of the hermeneutical approach has become somewhat inflated of late, to the point of seeming all-encompassing. And at that point hermeneutics does need to be relativized by a recalling of its own philosophic origins.[45]

In closing I would submit that the slighting of the critical among humanists and theologians is so recurrent a phenomenon as to constitute a pattern, and that the recognition of this pattern of neglect lays an imperative upon those who would do theology in the present world context. In principle there is no dichotomy of subject and object, in principle we are parts of a larger whole. But in point of fact we live in a world which is rent by oppression and alienation. The theologian must exercise exceeding great care lest the affirmation which is meant to engender vision instead invite a certain blindness, a sort of proleptic complacency. I am aware that my convictions in this regard have occasionally colored the exposition; particularly when I was striving to legitimate the critical over against the phenomenological, I may have been rather hard on humanistic psychology. I hope that the more balanced diagram which I have set forth may stand as an internal critic against the occasional excess. But I do believe that something along this line is the proper use of such a schema—to try to hear the questions which it puts against one's own position while appropriating it, nevertheless, to hammer out the word which one judges most needs to be spoken in the face of the present moment.

---

[45] Much of the power of Ricoeur's work may be attributed to his sensitivity to the transcendental context: witness the use of Hegel in *Freud and Philosophy* and the pervasive use of Kant. See Don Ihde, *Hermeneutic Phenomenology: The Philosophy of Paul Ricoeur* (Evanston: Northwestern University Press, 1971), pp. 59ff. Moreover his profound commitment to the discipline of the conceptual "detour" reflects a personal appropriation of the way of mediation; and conversely his abhorrence of premature cloture, the circle which reflection makes with itself, parallels the Frankfurt School's attack upon the philosophy of identity. But Ricoeur's detours are at the service of a certain notion of phenomenology, which indicates that the fundamental appeal is to a descriptive holism (cf. his frequent appeals to the "fullness" of symbolic language). Thus the critical moment does not attain to a significance in its own right and the consequent notion of the whole is, ironically, restrained.

CHAPTER FOUR
EVIL AND THE UNCONSCIOUS

*If it is not true that a divine
being fell, then we can only say
that one of the animals went entirely
off its head.*

G. K. Chesterton

The distinctiveness of the human—or, to follow Chesterton, the oddity of it—is the subject of the present essay. The question is classic and it is one to which the student of the humanities would seem to hold clear title. But the humanities in the modern age have found themselves thrown on the defensive by the claims of a scientific reductionism. Perhaps, so the suspicion runs, the humanist serves only to stutter out in a vague, poetic way the concepts science will one day enunciate with precision and finality. This spectre of scientism triumphant does much, I think, to explain the guarded fascination with which many humanists have been drawn to the field of psychology. Here in the science of the human mind one might hope to find a promising ally, a friend within the scientific camp.[1]

Psychology, from its side, has done much to encourage this hope. Indeed it has been at times the very voice of contemporary romanticism: it has promised to turn science to the task of opening up the depth dimension of experience; it has held out the vision of something more beyond the one-dimensional world of the positivist. The entire human potential movement within psychology is empowered by this vision. But, as the defense attorney says at a pivotal point in *The Brothers Karamazov,* psychology is "a knife that cuts both ways." For at any moment there may occur a bewildering reversal— psychology may turn upon the very aspiration which it has fostered. Suddenly psychology assumes the voice of the positivist, speaking now from within the fastness of human subjectivity. And from this vantage point it

---

[1] In this essay I treat "humanities" and "humanist" as cognate terms and assume that there are certain concerns which the theologian and humanist share. As a generalization one may say that in the time of the Enlightenment the theologian worried about reductionism while the humanist and the natural scientist (who were not sharply distinguished) did not. But by the twentieth century the lines had shifted: the humanist too had begun to worry about certain forms of reductionism and, not coincidentally, there was an increasing sociological division between scientist and humanist. It is this more recent state of affairs which the present essay presupposes.

proceeds to dissolve the longing for "something more" into "nothing more" than the twitching of a conditioned reflex or the self-deluded projection of a repressed libidinal desire. The results of this reversal are all about us in an all-too-knowing cynicism about the sources of human motivation.

Confronted with this turn of events, this mixed message from the side of psychology itself, the humanist has sought to make sense of things by ascribing the disparate voices to distinct schools or movements within psychology. Freud, for example, is commonly dismissed as a virtual positivist; one is encouraged to look elsewhere, perhaps to some form of humanistic psychology. This practice of segregating favorable and offending psychologies has become so much a part of the received wisdom that it may be said to have attained a ritualized form. One begins by praising Freud as the father of modern psychotherapy, then one proceeds to bury him for having remained a child of his times. The dismissal of Freud is confirmed by a few brisk references to his penchant for mechanistic metaphors such as "drive" and "energy," derived from the physics of his time. The aim of these references is precisely to evoke the spectre of reductionism, which then becomes sufficient warrant for turning from Freud to some more congenial alternative. As Freud himself lamented, "First they call me a genius and then they proceed to reject all my views."[2]

The unacknowledged effect of this commonplace strategy is to define the field of psychology and to prejudice certain options within psychology—all on the basis of one intense preoccupation, the anxiety about reductionism. I shall argue in the conclusion of the present essay that for all its virtues as an advocacy of the distinctively human, this defensive preoccupation has badly skewed our vision of things; indeed the preoccupation may verge on the pathological. For the present, however, it is enough to say that when we cut people out of the conversation, we deprive ourselves of the insights they may have to offer. Specifically I wish to argue that Freud still has much to teach us concerning this odd business of being human and that an effective way of engaging him in this regard is to bracket the question of reductionism and to approach him instead through the penetrating problem which Chesterton mentions, a problem which is an embarrassment to the upbeat world of popular psychology but an inescapable feature of any true confrontation with human experience: namely, the problem of evil.[3]

---

[2] Joseph Wortis, *Fragments of an Analysis with Freud* (New York: Simon and Schuster, 1954), p. 142. Freud's statement is quoted by Russell Jacoby, who gives several examples of the ritualized form; see Jacoby, *Social Amnesia: A Critique of Conformist Psychology from Adler to Laing* (Boston: Beacon Press, 1975), pp. 2-3.

[3] This alternative approach to Freud has strong precedent in the work of Paul Tillich and Reinhold Niebuhr. Influenced by existentialism, they found in Freud a powerful ally; particularly they underlined the Freudian awareness of human perversity, which effectively scuttled the Pelagian optimism inherited from the Enlightenment. But existentialism has declined in favor of late and as a result, it would seem, there has been less interest in the

Freud's contribution to this vital discussion may be explored under two headings familiar to the student of literature, the classic themes of *tragedy* and *self-delusion*. Thus, the present essay derives its structure: three sections on tragedy, two on self-delusion and a concluding section offering certain theological reflections. Further, each theme will be examined in the light of a recent movement within psychoanalysis: tragedy in light of the work of Heinz Kohut and certain precedents, and self-delusion in light of the work of the French psychoanalyst Jacques Lacan.[4] Thus, there is a secondary argument to the effect that certain current movements support a rehabilitation of our chosen themes. But this argument from currency will, I hope, remain secondary, for the field has been overrun by manifestoes, each acclaiming some movement simply because it was, for the moment, a novelty. Here it will be argued that the psychologies in question commend themselves precisely because their roots run deeper than the antinomies of fashion, attaining instead the subsoil of a certain creative orthodoxy. And especially will I wish to press this point with regard to the *unconscious*—for a proper reading of this protean concept is, I believe, the price of entry, the way of initiation, into the Freudian view of evil.

I

Were one to cast about in current American psychoanalysis for that movement which could best meet the test of a creative orthodoxy, the likely candidate might be certain theoretical advances on the subject of primary and secondary narcissism. The literature on this subject has come to popular attention through Christopher Lasch's recent book, *The Culture of Narcissism.* As Lasch observes, psychiatry has witnessed over the last twenty-five years the emergence of a peculiarly elusive, peculiarly contemporary sort of patient. "He does not suffer from debilitating fixations or phobias or from the conversion of repressed sexual energy into nervous ailments; instead he complains 'of vague, diffuse dissatisfactions with life' and feels his 'amorphous existence to be futile and purposeless.'" Marked by violent

---

approach to Freud which had been associated with that movement. Thus, the task of this essay must be to retrieve the *question* which existentialism discerned in Freud, by extricating the question from the precommitments of that particular philosophy. The task is to renew the discussion by reestablishing certain seemingly existentialist themes, most notably the themes of tragedy and self-delusion, on grounds more intrinsic to psychoanalysis. See Reinhold Niebuhr, "Human Creativity and Self-Concern in Freud's Thought," in *Freud and the Twentieth Century*, ed. Benjamin Nelson (New York: Meridian Books, 1957); Paul Tillich, "The Theological Significance of Existentialism and Psychoanalysis," in *The Theology of Culture* (New York: Oxford University Press, 1964).

[4] Thus, the discussion will be confined to Freud, and more specifically to certain of his recent commentators. It might well be fruitful to compare the results of this exploration, particularly as regards the concepts of the Imaginary and the Symbolic, with the thought of C. G. Jung.

oscillations of self-esteem and a penchant not for repression or sublimation but for "acting out," this pattern has only recently been canonized as that of the "border-line personality."[5]

Central to the research on the borderline personality is the work of Heinz Kohut, author of *The Analysis of the Self* and *The Restoration of the Self*. The case for Kohut's work as standing in the line of a creative orthodoxy may be made on the basis of a certain balance within his theoretical writings. On the one hand, Kohut speaks less of psychic mechanisms than of certain crucial experiences; in this he follows the lead of many neo-Freudian and post-Freudian revisionists. Yet at the same time he does retain the vocabulary of drive and instinct in a significant though secondary role. Similarly Kohut shares with the revisionists a skepticism about the centrality of the Oedipus complex. But heretofore those questioning the importance Freud attributed to this theory have generally done so in the name of subsequent growth and development; that Freud saw so much of the human drama as being played out in that early moment has seemed to many a heedless determinism, a blindness to choice and change. Kohut, for his part, is reserved in making such appeals to freedom; thus, he distances himself from the existentialists. Remarkably, his criticism of the Oedipus complex directs attention to developments which are not later, but *earlier*, making Kohut in this respect more Freudian than the Freudians.

I have noted that Kohut gives primacy to notions of "experience" and "self" in preference to notions of psychic mechanism. The argument for this primacy in theory is simple: he holds that the experience of the self has such primacy in reality. The first and fundamental demand of the child is not a demand for drive-satisfaction; it is rather a demand for a perfect empathy and oneness with its "self-object" (which is generally the mother).[6] Psychoanalysis itself, in its effort to explore these earliest experiences, must be aware of the depth of this demand for empathy (p. 306). Thus, to take the negative case, "whenever a patient reacts with rage to the analyst's interpretations," the reaction may be attributed to the fact that the patient experiences the analyst "from the point of view of the archaic self that has been activated in analysis," from which perspective the analyst appears as "a nonempathic attacker of the integrity of [the patient's] self" (p. 91). Accordingly,

> the analyst does not witness the emergence of a primary primitive-aggressive drive, he witnesses the disintegration of the preceding primary configuration, *the breakup of the primary self-experience* in

---

[5] Christopher Lasch, *The Culture of Narcissism: American Life in an Age of Diminishing Expectations* (New York: W. W. Norton, 1979), p. 37; a useful bibliographical survey is found on pp. 240–42.

[6] Heinz Kohut, *The Restoration of the Self* (New York: International Universities Press, 1977), p. 91; in the present section, reference to this work will be given parenthetically in the text.

which, in the child's perception, the child and the empathic self-object are one. (p. 91, emphasis added)

The crucial concept here is that of a primary self-experience and its dissolution.[7] For Kohut the breakup of this self-experience is the source of all that follows—including the so-called primary drives. Like many existential psychologists, Kohut contends that the patient's deepest anxiety is "the dread of the loss of his self—the fragmentation and estrangement from his body and mind in space, the breakup of his sense of continuity in time" (p. 105). But the existentialist generally discounts psychoanalytic drive theory as an inauthentic objectification of the self. In contrast, Kohut's creative orthodoxy lies in showing how a legitimate drive theory might be rescued within a coherent view of the self. On his view what happens in the case of certain pathologies is the following:

> It is the self of the child that, in consequence of the severely disturbed empathic responses of the parents, has not been securely established . . . that (in the attempt to reassure itself that it is alive, even that it exists at all) turns defensively toward pleasure aims through the stimulation of erogenic zones, and then, secondarily, brings about the oral (and anal) drive orientation. . . . (p. 74)

Thus Kohut can say, in a manner fit to confound traditionalist and revisionist alike, that "the intensity of the drive is not the cause of the central pathology . . . but its result" (p. 104).

From the vantage point of Kohut's theory it appears that contemporary culture may be experiencing a shift from the pathologies best described by classical psychoanalysis (e.g., obsessional neurosis) to "the pathology of the fragmented self" (so-called narcissistic disorders) and of the "depleted self" (the self devoid of ideals). The effect, in Kohut's terminology, is to replace the figure of "Guilty Man" with that of "Tragic Man" (pp. 238ff.)—a theme to which I shall return. In the face of this cultural landshift, Kohut places his hope in an early empathic merger through which parent communicates to infant an acceptance and celebration of our common lot as real but transient participants in the ongoing dance of life.

II

That Kohut should conclude on the theme of tragedy is evidence of the extent to which he succeeds in retaining the existentialist question while distancing himself from the concomitant answer. Indeed, Kohut's work is so

---

[7] Kohut's treatment of the primary self-experience may be supplemented by reference to the discussion of the "normal symbiotic phase" in Margaret S. Mahler, Fred Pine, and Anni Bergman, *The Psychological Birth of the Human Infant: Symbiosis and Individuation* (New York: Basic Books, 1975), pp. 43–51.

much to the point that I have been at pains to indicate that his is a movement which would have to be reckoned with in its own right, indepen-
dently of its peculiar fit with our preoccupations. Before proceeding to a
discussion of this providential congruence, however, I wish to introduce
another figure whose thought may be set alongside that of Kohut. This is
Norman O. Brown, the author of *Life Against Death* (1959) and *Love's Body*
(1966). In the eyes of many, Brown's work belongs at the opposite pole of
respectability from that of Kohut, by virtue of its having been appropriated
by the enthusiasts of the erstwhile greening of America. Yet I wish to suggest that one may bracket Brown's utopianism and that what remains, if
one does so, is a remarkably trenchant account of the human condition
drawn from a close reading of the Freudian corpus.[8] Thus, I propose to
retain Kohut as a standard by which to select from Brown, while adopting
Brown as a device by which to expand upon the implications of Kohut.

Approached in this manner, Brown's *Life Against Death* displays certain
parallels to Kohut's attempt to fashion a creative orthodoxy. Kohut, we may
recall, seeks to clear a path between a *reductionism* which would speak solely
in terms of drives and instincts and a *revisionism* which would speak solely
in terms of self and experience. One might further add that such reductionism is characteristically intent upon the commonalities which unite the
animal with the human while the revisionist tends, in contrast, to seize
upon the distinctively human. One would then be in a position to appreciate Brown's programmatic statement that "we need, in fine, a metaphysic
which recognizes both the continuity between man and the animals and
also the discontinuity."[9]

Moreover, like Kohut, Brown looks to the infant's earliest experience.
He takes as his point of departure the ethnological observation that, whatever else may go into forming the distinctively human, one determinative
factor is surely the extended period of protection and nurturance which is
accorded the human infant (pp. 24ff.). This formative period of protection
may be summarized in two related terms: *dependence* and *gratification*. (Brown
makes much of the family in this connection, so it is important to note that
on my broad formulation of it, such protection is independent of any particular family arrangement short of base neglect. Human nurturance is even
independent of human parenting; in principle it might possibly be effected

---

[8] Here as elsewhere my intent is to allow the critical moment to have its say without
limiting it in an a priori or external fashion. There is the possibility that a version of
Brown's utopian thinking might be reintroduced in connection with the Symbolic, discussed
below; cf. Norman O. Brown, *Love's Body* (New York: Random House, 1966).

[9] Norman O. Brown, *Life Against Death: The Psychoanalytical Meaning of History* (New York:
Random House, 1959), p. 83; in this section, references to this work will be given parenthetically in the text. For a feminist argument which confirms Brown's analysis on a number of
points, see Dorothy Dinnerstein, *The Mermaid and the Minotaur* (New York: Harper and Row,
1976).

by an artificial environment. But it seems that in every case imaginable there would have to be protection which would perdure for an extended period, with all that entails of dependence and gratification. Otherwise one would have a sort of "wild child" who would suffer such emotional damage as might stunt its very humanity.)

So, a period of protection is indispensable for the founding of those qualities of creativity, meaning and love which the humanistic psychologist so rightly celebrates. But now let us pause to note one point quite carefully, for the effect of this same period of nurturance is, by its very nature, to place the infant in a fundamental bind. Note first that protection gives gratification; there would be little point to it, did it not. And gratification which is protected and thus encouraged to luxuriate gives rise to desires and fantasies of a very specific sort: "sheltered from reality by parental care, infantile sexuality—Eros or the life instinct—conceives *the dream of narcissistic omnipotence* in a world of love and pleasure" (p. 113, emphasis added). Note further that at the same time and just as inevitably, protection presupposes and fosters dependence; there would be little need for it, did it not. And sheltered dependence generates desires and fantasies which are of quite another sort: "objective dependence on parental care creates in the child *a passive, dependent need to be loved,* which is just the opposite of his dream of narcissistic omnipotence" (p. 113, emphasis added). Thus, at the wellspring of our humanity Brown discerns two desires, as uncompromising as they are contradictory. They are as fundamental as the human cries of "Hold me!" and "Let me go!" The result is what Freud calls, in a deceptively simple phrase, "the conflict of ambivalence" (p. 113).

The conflict of desire and desire, taken at another angle, is a conflict of desire and reality. The reality is the fact of dependence and the correlative fact of the mother's *otherness.* It is brought home to the infant by a crisis which even the most scrupulous protectiveness cannot postpone forever: the experience of *separation.* Whether we imagine this separation as occurring at birth or at some later moment, whether we conceive it as a particular experience or as the paradigm of many, it remains "the prototype of psychic traumas, the experience of wanting but not being able to find the mother . . ." (p. 114). The dark secret of the sheer obduracy of reality crashes upon a consciousness which stands defenseless before it. Suddenly the mother is no longer an extension of my will—what then of my omnipotence? Suddenly the mother is separate—what then of my need? The moment she ceases to fill my field of vision, I glimpse behind her the larger backdrop, the cold, abiding reality of an inattentive cosmos. And if this sounds unduly philosophic, the infant's anxiety is not. For, "because the child loves the mother so much . . . it feels separation from the mother as death" (p. 115). And separation felt as death feeds an anxiety which is "both a flight from death and a death experience" (p. 114). As in a nightmare in which one runs but does not move, the child is ensnared by its very fear.

And so in some inchoate way it seeks to come to terms: it will buy off the final death by inflicting a provisional death upon itself. This is the moment of pathos and surrender which we conveniently obscure by the abstract term "repression." The reality—like that of the animal which escapes the trap by gnawing off its leg—is an act of psychic self-mutilation.

Though Freud underscored the significance of this act by calling it *primal* repression, it is a concept which many writers have preferred to disregard.[10] One reason for this neglect, perhaps, is the concept's elusive logic; it is, I wish to suggest, a logic of *differentiation*.[11] For primal repression, unlike the subsequent acts which are repression in the customary sense of the term, does not simply transfer materials to a clearly preexistent unconscious. The act is distinguished by the fact that it is posited so far back in the infant's development that it does not so much presuppose the unconscious as create it. That is to say, the infant moves from a condition in which the psyche is neither clearly conscious nor clearly unconscious, but of a single relatively undifferentiated state, to a condition in which conscious and unconscious have become relatively differentiated, and even antipathetic.

A similar logic of differentiation obtains when one turns from the repressing to the repressed. Brown postulates that in the animal's experience life instinct and death instinct interact relatively freely. Eros, the impetus to union, and Thanatos, the impetus to destruction, "fuse" in some cases and alternate in others, and through these permutations they constitute the natural rhythm of animal existence. With the human this ceases to be the case. "Man is distinguished from animals by having separated, ultimately into a state of mutual conflict, aspects of life (instincts) which in animals exist in some condition of undifferentiated unity or harmony" (p. 83). At this point the reader is apt to assume that the infant represses the awareness which is allied to one instinct, the awareness of death or separation, but retains in consciousness the other awareness, namely the life instinct, the appetite for survival. But the life instinct as Freud understood it is more primitive than the notion of the survival of a differentiated self. The primal form of Eros is the infant's desire for union with its object and this impulse too falls victim to primary repression. For the infant, having repressed its awareness of the object, can hardly afford to entertain the memory of how vehemently the object was desired. Certainly the infant does proceed as if life could be affirmed and death denied—that is a fair definition of its effort

---

[10] Peter Madison, *Freud's Concept of Repression and Defense, Its Theoretical and Observational Language* (Minneapolis: University of Minnesota Press, 1961), p. 89. Cf. Marie Jahoda, *Freud and the Dilemmas of Psychology* (New York: Basic Books, 1977).

[11] This logic remains constant whether the occurrence of primal repression be located at birth, as in the thought of Otto Rank, or be located thereafter, or whether it be taken as a collective notion designating a series of actual occurrences. On these latter questions the research of Mahler, Pine and Bergman, cited earlier, is most significant.

at omnipotence and immortality. But the life instinct like the death instinct is now beyond its reach, cast into a penumbral sphere where life and death both recede in a barren dialectic.

Trying to choose definitively, the child succumbs to a pattern of endless indecision. Trying to expel certain realities, it polarizes the possibilities. And all its subsequent ventures, founded upon this first repression, confirm the original pattern. Each abortive solution becomes in turn a problem; repression secures nothing but insecurity, and anxiety thrust from view is at liberty to diffuse like a subterranean pollution till it emerges as the stuff of human experience. Thus, "the infantile conflict between actual impotence and dreams of omnipotence" becomes "the basic theme of the universal history of mankind" (p. 25). The argument is sweeping but it all hinges on a single point, the concept of primal repression. This neglected, contested notion furnishes the bridge between Brown's title and his subtitle: between the conflict of "life against death" and the effort to articulate "the psychoanalytical meaning of history."

III

From Kohut's clinical reflection to Brown's world-historical speculation there is a distance of substance and of style. But the differences, I wish to suggest, make it the more remarkable that two such disparate approaches should so agree upon the necessity of retrieving the concept of primal repression or, in Kohut's distinctive terms, "the breakup of the primary self-experience." Let us begin with the general picture which Kohut and Brown give of the unconscious and then proceed to the theme of tragedy.

We may resume our discussion of the unconscious by returning to the search for a creative orthodoxy capable of steering between the reductionist and revisionist pitfalls. On the face of it these latter positions would seem to be polar opposites. The reductionist endorses the Freudian unconscious and pursues the notion with unflinching consistency, while the revisionist rejects the Freudian proposal in a manner which is no less adamant. But in the *image* they have of this disputed notion, in their interpretation of the concept of the Freudian unconscious, the disputants are remarkably agreed. Both regard the Freudian unconscious in dualistic fashion as the quasi-volcanic irruption of an underlying animality: our suppressed animality slips the leash, visiting disorder upon human affairs.

The achievement of Kohut and Brown is the alternative they provide in the face of this uninspired consensus. Kohut sees our instinct as arising from, or at least as being crucially aggravated by, certain originary experiences. Brown sees our unconscious as arising from, or at least as being crucially differentiated by, the very condition of infantile dependence which makes possible our distinctive humanity. Taken together they make it imaginable that the Freudian unconscious is the function *not* of some residual animality, *but of our distinctive humanity!* Language, for example, is in many ways an index of human transcendence. But to learn to speak the child needs an extensive period of creative playfulness, a period of fantasy, mimicry and babble; and we have seen how this same period of playful and protected fantasy produces, by an inexorable logic, the familiar constellation of human neurosis.

From another angle, we may say that the reductionist holds to a naturalistic concept of instinct and a mechanistic view of instinctual conflict; and that the revisionist, repelled by this crude doctrine, seeks an alternative to its naturalism. In the course of this necessary reconstruction regarding the *nature* of the instinct, however, the revisionist tends to assume, as if it were a necessary concomitant, an uncritically sanguine view of instinctual *conflict.* In this light the distinctiveness of Kohut and Brown would be that with them the concept of instinct is indeed revised but the degree of conflict remains undiminished, thus puncturing a certain gratuitous optimism. Indeed, for Kohut and Brown the conflict is actually intensifed, and once again the reason has to do with the distinctively human. Here we may read a second time with a different emphasis the earlier passage from Brown: "Man is distinguished from animals by having separated, ultimately into a state of mutual conflict, aspects of life (instincts) which in animals exist in some condition of undifferentiated unity or harmony." The distinctive is precisely the instigation of this conflict.

To summarize, earliest infancy may be understood as an indissoluble interplay of experience and fantasy: what Kohut speaks of as the "primary self-experience" and what Brown refers to as the dreams of omnipotence and love. This interplay expands and luxuriates in the prolonged and protected infancy which is necessarily accorded the human child. In proportion as this has happened, the child must experience separation as deeply traumatic, a sort of death, and that trauma imparts to the entire life an abiding disequilibrium. In its broad contours this view of human development seems to me to commend itself by its simplicity. It takes its point of departure in no unreflective dualism of the animal and the distinctively human, but posits rather a more circumspect duality. Thus, the theory is not constrained to introduce further hypotheses to account for how it is that the apparent incommensurables can interrelate; it is rather able to attend to the process of polarization as it unfolds within the abiding dyad. This conceptual elegance, reinforced by the evidences of a creative orthodoxy and by the widespread recognition which has been accorded to Kohut if not to Brown, may be warrant enough for adopting the position as a viable option among the various readings of psychoanalysis.

My own concern is to relate this technical theory of the unconscious to the general theme of tragedy—and the necessary first step in making this connection is to spell out what may be meant by "the tragic." The accepted form in discussions of tragedy is to begin by lamenting the contemporary usage which so debases the classical meaning of the term. I too wish to adopt an understanding of the classical usage as normative; but at the same time I would submit that the popular usage, which bestows the term so liberally upon reversals of any magnitude, may still carry within it the residue of an ancient and important perspective. The popular reflex is to speak of "a tragedy" on any occasion when one witnesses the destruction of a human good and when one does so with a feeling of helplessness. Helplessness entails a sense of the inexorable, and in this fashion it may evoke the ancient gnostic vision of scattered embers of light assaulted by the encroaching darkness: of the frailty of human values existing at the mercy of a hostile or indifferent cosmos. One need only consider the existentialist movement to recognize that this dualistic vision continues as a part of the modern sensibility. And yet I do not wish fully to identify tragedy with this vision, even if shorn of the promise of gnostic salvation. Rather I wish to suggest that a key to the contemporary relevance of classical tragedy may be found in the fact that such dualism constitutes a sort of limit possibility toward which classic tragedy continually inclines—and which it continually seeks to transcend.

The interplay of inclination and resistance may be observed in the classical understanding of the tragic situation. Roy Schafer has pointed to Max Scheler's concept of "'*the tragic knot,*' which expresses 'the entanglement between the creation and destruction of a value'; by this he refers to the coinciding . . . in one quality, power or ability, of the influences that both champion the value and destroy it."[12] Thus, tragedy resists the dualistic conviction that the conflict is a foreign impingement, the crushing of human value by a cosmic juggernaut. Rather the conflict is located within the world of human values; it is in effect a conflict between good and good. By so much, tragedy transcends the dualistic vision. Yet for that very reason the conflict proves the more compelling, the more rooted within the human—the more inevitable; and in this fashion the spectre of dualism reasserts itself. Similarly, when one approaches classical tragedy from the side of the protagonist, one is struck that the individual is portrayed as caught up in events and yet responsible for them. There is a certain givenness to the situation, a certain *facticity*; and yet the tragic figure is somehow responsible, there is a certain *complicity*. In the labyrinthine interplay of facticity and complicity, tragedy again approaches dualism and yet resists it.

Now we are in a position to link tragedy and psychoanalysis in a fairly specific way; let us return once more to the theory of the unconscious. Ernest Becker, in *The Denial of Death,* has done much to reacquaint popular psychology with the realities of tragedy and self-delusion. But it is significant that Becker's own vision of the human condition is avowedly dualistic;

---

[12] Roy Schafer, *A New Language for Psychoanalysis* (New Haven: Yale University Press, 1976), pp. 36–37, emphasis added; Scheler, in turn, is drawing upon Hegel.

indeed, on Becker's view the dualism *is* the tragedy.[13] The plight is that we are spirits bound to a mortal body: we are, in Becker's vivid phrase, "gods with anuses."[14] And the anuses are not immortal. This vision of freedom mired in finitude is strikingly reminiscent of Jean-Paul Sartre; thus, one is forced to acknowledge that in Becker the existentialist penetration regarding Freud's question continues to be compromised by the presuppositions of the existentialist psychology. The fundamental premise for the unconscious continues to be the intrusion into human affairs of any underlying physicality or animality. Despite his many compelling insights, Becker provides a further illustration of the irony that existentialism, for all its insistence upon temporality, directs the discussion of the human condition toward an eternal, quasi-natural given.

Freud himself is more complex. One can discern even in his naturalistic language an effort to do justice to the sheer givenness of the unconscious—the sheer resistance of it, if you will—and yet to view it, nevertheless, as fundamentally historical![15] Moreover, this history is portrayed as a story which, though it has unfolded with a certain inevitability, yet displays the marks of the individual's active complicity. Here, I would submit, is the effective link between psychoanalysis and tragedy. It is because of his understanding of the unconscious that Freud sees the psychoanalytic situation as one of a conflict of values, a "tragic knot." The very history which gives the gifts of human distinctiveness also fosters human neurosis. And it is because of his understanding of the unconscious that Freud sees the individual's role as a tangled web of facticity and complicity. The existentialist, in contrast, is finally at one with the dualist in attempting to base the human condition directly upon certain primitive givens, without the mediating terms which can only be supplied by a concrete history. The result is, in the name of tragedy, to eviscerate the tragic dynamic—to dissolve the dialectic between the dualistic vision and a continuous and equally indispensable effort to transcend it.

IV

If the American rethinking of Freud centers upon the work of Kohut and his associates, the search for a movement of comparable import in Europe must look to the influence of structuralism and specifically to the "French Freud" of Jacques Lacan and his circle.[16] The testimonies to the

---

[13] E.g., Becker, *The Denial of Death* (New York: The Free Press, 1973), p. 30.

[14] Ibid., p. 51.

[15] This point is developed below; cf. Paul Ricoeur, "The Question of Proof in Freud's Psychoanalytic Writings," in *The Philosophy of Paul Ricoeur: An Anthology of His Work,* ed. C. E. Reagen and D. Stewart (Boston: Beacon Press, 1978).

[16] Lacan's essays have been collected as *Ecrits* (Paris: Editions du Seuil, 1966); in the present essay references are to the English translation of a portion of this work: Lacan, *Écrits:*

significance of this movement are commonly coupled, however, with expressions of dismay at the hermetic character which the movement has assumed. The vocabulary is arcane, the leader is needlessly elusive, and the postulant seeking instruction is required, by way of initiation, to master the writings of the linguist Ferdinand de Saussure and the anthropologist Claude Lévi-Strauss.[17] For our own purposes we may dispense with these rites of entrance and exclusion. What is needed is simply a sampling of Lacanian thought to serve as evidence that the movement merits further study.

Let us begin, then, with something fairly concrete. In the early pages of *Beyond the Pleasure Principle* Freud recounts a simple game, a form of peek-a-boo, played by a child of one-and-a-half years. A commentator, Anika Lemaire, summarizes the episode.

> The child, whose favourite game is recounted by Freud, had a cottonreel with a piece of string tied around it. Holding the string, he would throw the reel over the edge of his curtained cot. While doing so he uttered a prolonged 'ooh,' which was easily interpreted as being an attempt at the German *fort*, meaning 'gone' or 'away.' He would then pull the reel back into his field of vision, greeting its reappearance with a joyful *da* ('there'). It should be noted that the child's mother, busy outside, was in the habit of leaving her son alone for long periods.
>
> The game thus had the signification of a renunciation. It allowed this 18-month-old child to bear without protest the painful lived experience of his mother's alternating disappearance and reappearance. By means of this game in which he repeated with an object—the reel and the string—the coming and going of his mother, the child assumed an active part in the event, thus ensuring his domination of it.[18]

This incident is of cardinal importance for Lacan; his writings return to it time and again. Remarkably, it picks up the child's story at just the point where our discussion of Brown left off, with the struggle to deal with the

---

A Selection, trans. Alan Sheridan (New York: W. W. Norton, 1977). A fairly nontechnical introduction is Anika Lemaire, *Jacques Lacan* (London: Routledge and Kegan Paul, 1977). For closer study the indispensable guides are two textual commentaries: Anthony Wilden, *The Language of the Self* (Baltimore: Johns Hopkins Press, 1968) and the volume by John P. Muller and William J. Richardson, *Lacan Interpreted: A Reader's Guide to Selected Texts* (New York: International Universities Press, 1980). For social-historical context see Sherry Turkle, *Psychoanalytic Politics: Freud's French Revolution* (New York: Basic Books, 1978).

[17] See Anthony Wilden, *System and Structure: Essays in Communication and Exchange* (London: Tavistock Publications, 1972), pp. 462ff, for a critical analysis of Lacan.

[18] Lemaire, *Jacques Lacan*, pp. 51–52. Sigmund Freud, *The Standard Edition of the Complete Psychological Works of Sigmund Freud*, trans. under editorship of James Strachey, 24 vols. (London: Hogarth Press, 1959), 18:14ff. Cf. Lacan, *Ecrits*, pp. 103–4; Wilden, *Language*, pp. 152–54, 163–64.

mother's absence. The incident's fascination for Lacan is the fact that the child copes with the separation by using language (indeed by a very early use of language); and conversely, that language is thereby implicated, at its very origins, in the interplay of presence and absence. By means of the alternation the child relativizes the absence; by naming the absence at all, the child assumes a certain mastery over it. All this, we may say, is gain. But at the same time, the child has involved itself in a language, and thus in a linguistic structure, which far exceeds its grasp, which leads it knows not where. And further the child has settled for a substitute gratification. In all this there is loss and estrangement, and thus we have a clue to the meaning of the oft-quoted Lacanian maxim that the unconscious is structured like a language.

But one must be wary of any single maxim; if the *Fort! Da!* so fascinates Lacan, it is because its meaning is multivalent. Specifically, the incident serves as point of intersection for three distinct psychoanalytic perspectives which Lacan describes (albeit somewhat opaquely) as "the Real," "the Imaginary" and "the Symbolic." Let us consider these one by one. Of the first, the *Real*, Lacan has the least to say; but what he does say is enough to indicate that the term does not designate any commonsense object. Anika Lemaire suggests that the Real may represent Lacan's appropriation of the phenomenological concept of "lived experience," a naive, spontaneous awareness of the world about us. Further, Lemaire suggests that for Lacan this awareness has been repressed. "Always seeking to 'rationalize,' to 'repress' the lived experience, reflection will eventually become profoundly divergent from that lived experience."[19] This observation is elevated beyond the level of a commonplace about alienation thanks to the specifically psychoanalytic premise that the repressed experience is complex, including the trauma of separation as well as the experience which preceded that occurrence (cf. the fact that both Thanatos and Eros are repressed, according to Brown). To understand this process of repression one is driven once again to a logic of relative differentiation; and, as in the discussion of Brown, one discovers that unconscious and conscious emerge not as sequential stages but as correlative occurrences, the reciprocal products of a single process of differentiation. Thus, we may say that the significance of the Real for Lacan's understanding of the unconscious is that the Real represents the abiding presence of a complex, repressed awareness.

The second dimension is that of the *Imaginary*. It represents the limit case of differentiation, namely a condition of *opposition*. The Imaginary is the birthplace of the ego, the sense of a distinctive self, as the infant increasingly defines itself over against its surroundings. But the emergence of self is in fact inseparable from the child's relationship to certain significant others. Indeed, the very notion of autonomy first confronts the child from

---

[19] Lemaire, *Jacques Lacan*, p. 53; cf. Lacan, *Ecrits*, p. 216.

"out there," embodied in the other person; and as a result there is generated
an Imaginary dialectic of narcissism and identification which is fed relent-
lessly by the child's perception of the gulf that lies between that image of
sublime self-possession and the child's own interior confusion and incompleteness.[20] In an alternative theory which has much the same effect, René
Girard postulates that we find our selves by mimicry and that mimicry,
whereby I imitate the other's desire for a particular object, leads inevitably to
competition and conflict. The situation finds its paradigm in the conflict of
siblings from Cain and Abel, through Romulus and Remus struggling within
the womb, to Shem and Shaun of *Finnegan's Wake*.[21] Whatever the depiction,
the logic is constant: two combatant figures confined within a closed system.
In Lemaire's phrase, it is a logic of "immediate opposition"; and Lacan's
contention is, in effect, that it will remain a logic of opposition as long as it
remains immediate.[22] On Lacan's view the aim of analysis is to open the
system by introducing, in the person of the therapist, a third figure who will
not play the mirroring game. But as long as the situation remains one of
mirroring, the subject can fantasize control; and as long as the subject is bent
on control, he or she will refuse to surrender the seeming advantage of a
system which is closed. The articulation of this self-appropriated bind is the
contribution of the Imaginary to an understanding of the unconscious.

The third dimension is that of the *Symbolic*. It is the realm of language,
which, by virtue of its systematic character, may be taken as a paradigm of
the entire social order. Lacan thus speaks of language as a structure and of
the unconscious as exhibiting, like language, the essential devices of metaphor and metonymy. But Lacan also approaches language by way of a
Heideggerian distinction between language which is inauthentic or "empty"
and language which is authentic or "full." The relating of these two quite
disparate perspectives, the structuralist and the Heideggerian, is determinative for Lacan's notion of the Symbolic.[23] The Imaginary tries to *use* language rather than participate in it; it treats language as a closed system
which may be manipulated to serve the subject's need for omnipotence and
evasion, and the result corresponds to Heidegger's concept of idle chatter,
the empty word. But a closed system cannot liberate, it can only mirror
one's self-enclosure. The Symbolic, in contrast, requires submission to an
open system which exceeds the subject's grasp. The Imaginary regards the
openness of language as a threat and submission to language as defeat.
Accordingly the figure of the Father—embodying language, law and social

---

[20] See Lacan's theory of the "*stade du miroir*," *Ecrits*, pp. 1–7; Wilden, *Language*, pp. 159–61.

[21] René Girard, *Violence and the Sacred* (Baltimore: The Johns Hopkins Press, 1977), pp.
169ff. Cf. Lacan, pp. 25–29; Wilden, *Language*, pp. 164–65. It is fitting that both Girard and
Brown cite the same powerful lines from Auden's "Vespers": see the interview with Girard
in *Diacritics* (Spring 1978), p. 54; Brown, *Love's Body*, pp. 26–27.

[22] Lemaire, *Jacques Lacan*, p. 60.

[23] Lacan, *Ecrits*, pp. 40ff.

order—becomes the ultimate rival. This for Lacan is the meaning of the Oedipus complex: it represents a further, more savage reenactment of the original Imaginary bind. Thus, Lacan can say that a sort of castration, a surrendering of one's fantasy of omnipotent self-sufficiency, is the price of admission to the fullness of the Word.[24] The vision of this tragic liberation, never completed and always at stake, is the Symbolic's contribution to an understanding of the unconscious.

V

Lacan's treatment of each of these spheres is sufficiently suggestive that there is a temptation to seize upon some one of the three, taken in isolation, as the key to the unconscious. But as we noted earlier, Lacan's approach is multivalent; the key lies not in any one of the three but in certain specific interactions among them. Thus, for example, the unconscious does not lie in the lived experience of an untroubled Real, but in a process of differentiation within the Real which already bears the imprint of Imaginary bifurcation. Nor is the unconscious to be found in Imaginary opposition per se, apart from the memory of the repressed Real; nor in the language of the Symbolic per se, apart from the Imaginary resistance to that system. Once it is understood in this fashion, Lacan's account of the unconscious articulates with our earlier discussion of tragedy. There is the "tragic knot": the ego, the seat of the distinctively human, is simultaneously a defensive construct, an Imaginary effort after an impossible self-sufficiency. There is the interweaving of facticity and complicity: the situation is not of the child's making, yet the Imaginary project is undeniably the child's own fantasy. As with classic tragedy, the picture here is pervaded by a certain inevitability; and yet at the same time there is, in and through that sense of inevitability, an enlivening resistance to the dualistic fatalism that would seem to follow from it. Nor is this resistance to be dismissed as an accident of temperament. Lacan's every treatment of the Imaginary provides an implicit critique of any dualistic fetish; indeed, his work is defined by the effort to fashion a psychology which is not itself subject to Imaginary misconstruction.

Blindness begets tragedy, tragedy unacknowledged perpetuates further deception, and through it all there is a tacit complicity, such that deception becomes self-deception as well. Our discussion of tragedy already gives us purchase on the theme of self-delusion. But Freud, particularly as rendered by Lacan, may allow us to be somewhat more specific; three points are of particular interest. First, note that the tragic reality which is unacknowledged is a certain separation; and note that the effect of this denial, embodied in Lacan's Imaginary, is a whole way of being in the world, namely a

---

[24] Ibid., pp. 281-91. For a thoughtful appropriation of Lacan from a feminist perspective, see Juliet Mitchell, *Psychoanalysis and Feminism* (New York: Random House, 1974), pp. 382-98.

posture of (identification and) opposition. Implicit here is Lacan's distinctive turn upon a central Freudian notion, the return of the repressed, which is also the crucial link between tragedy and self-delusion. It is, in brief, that *separation, once repressed, returns as opposition.*[25]

The other two points elaborate this central irony. Looking backward, as it were, one may say that *opposition is the loss of difference.* By the notion of "difference" I mean to suggest the diffuse, qualitative variety of the child's earliest lived experience. The suggestion is an alternative to those who hold that there is no awareness of difference for the child in its earliest state or that the earliest consciousness represents a sort of absolute subjectivity. After all, the child does perceive, however globally, and it is probably nearer the mark to say that the child perceives differences, albeit in a relatively undifferentiated state. Such awareness, which may continue as the substratum of our lived experience, honors a logic other than that of opposition. Anthony Wilden, one of Lacan's most interesting commentators, speaks of "analogical" knowledge, exemplified in one's sense of the contours of a terrain, in contrast to "digital" knowledge, exemplified in one's ability to punctuate a terrain with boundaries and property lines.[26] Once the lines become of primary importance, as they do in the case of technology, one loses the richness of innocent difference and the stage is set for Imaginary opposition. Here is basis for a legitimate critique of "instrumental reason." But difference is lost in another respect as well, for it is a commonplace that the longer one remains locked in mirrorlike combat, the more one comes to resemble that which one opposes—the more it is the case that one can no longer tell the difference. In such a world identification and anger dance endlessly, the shadows of an immediate opposition.

Difference and otherness are denied by virtue of their association with the experience of separation, and the price paid for this denial is immersion in a fatal dialectic of opposition. Conversely, with due regard to the ever tenuous and incomplete character of the process, one may say that *entry into the Symbolic is the restoration of difference.* The telos of analysis is commonly portrayed in terms of wholeness and ego strength, but for Lacan such notions surrender psychology to the very fantasies it must combat.[27] Paul Ricoeur is closer when he speaks of the aim of analysis as an *amor fati*, an affirmation of implacable fate; this is a fitting statement of Freud's kinship with tragedy. Closer still, perhaps, is the marvelous dictum implied by Roy Schafer: that analysis may begin in melodrama, proceed to tragedy, and

[25] In the present section I venture well beyond Lacan's explicit formulations. My suggestions are heavily indebted to Wilden, *System and Structure*; see particularly pp. 125ff., 145ff. On the concept of "difference," see Gregory Bateson, *Mind and Nature* (New York: E. P. Dutton, 1979), pp. 94ff.

[26] Wilden, *System and Structure*, pp. 155ff.; to Wilden's "analogical" knowledge compare Lemaire's interpretation of the Real as lived experience.

[27] Lacan, *Ecrits*, pp. 230-31.

possibly, just possibly, arrive at some glimpse of the comic vision.[28] Melodrama—what better term for the Imaginary script wherein I, the blameless
hero, am pitted against a world of uncomprehending evil? And tragedy—
the relentless moment when I do confront the enemy and discover that it
is I. But also, just possibly, a certain comedy—for as Saul Bellow has said in
a similar context, "there may be some truths which are, after all, our friends
in the universe." Ricoeur himself implies as much in speaking of Freud's
implicit teleology; Freud the stoic must not be divorced from the Freud
whose achievement W. H. Auden characterized in these lines:

> . . . as they lie in the grass of our neglect,
>   So many long-forgotten objects
>   Revealed by his undiscouraged shining
> Are returned to us and made precious again;
> Games we had thought we must drop as we grew up,
>   Little noises we dared not laugh at,
>   Faces we made when no one was looking.

It is in this fashion that one may speak, however cautiously, of a Freudian
eschatology.[29]

VI

"The theory of repression is the corner-stone on which the whole structure of psychoanalysis rests."[30] This line from Freud is quoted frequently
and yet, ironically, the concept of *primal* repression continues to be widely
neglected. The present essay has sought to correct this situation by arguing
that if repression is important to an understanding of the human condition,
primal repression is important *a fortiori*. Now to round off the argument I
wish to consider some implications which our Freudian exploration may
have for certain humanistic concerns. But throughout the discussion the
concerns of the humanities have been viewed in such a way that they may
overlap with those of theology; and it is toward theology of one sort or
another that the problem of evil presses us. Therefore, I propose to focus

---

[28] Schafer, *New Language for Psychoanalysis,* pp. 22–56.

[29] W. H. Auden, "In Memory of Sigmund Freud" in *Collected Shorter Poems 1930–1944* (London: Faber and Faber, 1950), p. 174. Ricoeur joins Brown and Lacan in characterizing the
goal as an accession to the fullness of language: Ricoeur, *The Conflict of Interpretations: Essays in
Hermeneutics* (Evanston: Northwestern University Press, 1974), pp. 192–95, cf. pp. 455–49.
This is not to say that the unconscious is *only* a matter of language, nor is it to say that the
goal is readily attainable. If we press too hard and too soon to know how close the goal may
be, we deflect our attention from the tragic discipline which is necessary in order to know
the direction at all—and we are apt to collapse Freud once again into a revisionist psychology which is fundamentally alien to him.

[30] Freud, *Standard Edition,* 14:16.

this concluding section by proceeding with theology in the foreground and the humanities in the near background.[31]

A point of entry is provided by the classical theological distinction between *moral* evil and *natural* evil. Moral evil is distinguished by the fact that it requires some deliberate human action or at least some human intention; natural evil does not. The child abuse which torments Ivan in *The Brothers Karamazov* is a moral evil; the Lisbon earthquake which was so critical for Voltaire is a natural evil. Applying this distinction to our own thematic, we find that acts of self-delusion gravitate in the direction of moral evil while the circumstances of tragedy point us, at least in part, toward a consideration of natural evil. I propose to pursue these points of connection and to do so with reference to three movements or worldviews which have had particular impact upon our modern consciousness: namely psychoanalysis, existentialism, and the Enlightenment.

The Enlightenment is of interest because it stands in such pointed contrast to the more recent positions. For the Enlightenment, natural evil tended to be equated with evil in nature. Cosmic evil was a sort of residual drag, the inertia of recalcitrant matter; and like matter, it was a thing to be subdued. The optimism of the Enlightenment survives into the present, often as a tranquilizing accompaniment to the ravages of technology; but now it is juxtaposed with a distinctly modern or postmodern anguish—a reassertion of the tragic. The historian Gerald Izenberg has described psychoanalysis and existentialism as the twin agencies by which the Enlightenment confidence in human autonomy was cast into a state of extended crisis.[32] For psychoanalysis and for existentialism, natural evil resides not in physical nature but in the nature of things. That is to say, it is not a remediable problem, a puzzle to be resolved, but a tragic knot in which creation and destruction are indissolubly fused. Nor is humanity an exception to this order of things, the ordained solution to this cosmic flaw, as the Enlightenment believed; rather the effect of the human is to distill the tragedy into another, more intense form. As regards natural evil, therefore, psychoanalysis and existentialism stand together over against the Enlightenment tradition; and it is fitting that Paul Tillich and Reinhold Niebuhr, two theologians who have been instructed by existentialism, should concur that in their opposition to the Enlightenment gospel of salvation through self-improvement, psychoanalysis is their ally.

But if the tragic vision is reborn in this century, it reappears in a distinctive mode. It appears under the sign of what Paul Ricoeur has called

---

[31] Regarding the relationship between theology and the humanities assumed in the present essay, cf. Paul Ricoeur, "Philosophical Hermeneutics and Theological Hermeneutics," *Studies in Religion/Sciences Religieuses* 5:1 (Toronto: University of Toronto Press, 1975).

[32] Gerald N. Izenberg, *The Existentialist Critique of Freud: The Crisis of Autonomy* (Princeton: Princeton University Press, 1976).

"the hermeneutic of suspicion," which itself derives from the Hegelian concept of false consciousness. Psychoanalysis and existentialism thus continue to be strikingly parallel as regards our second theme, their respective dissections of self-delusion. Both trace the tragic flaw to a divided consciousness which simultaneously admits and refuses the realities of estrangement; and further, both expose a pattern of behavior which inadvertently dramatizes the very obsession it would deny. If such patterns of self-delusion provide a key to moral evil, then with regard to moral evil as with regard to natural evil, the alignment of psychoanalysis and existentialism over against the Enlightenment continues to hold.

Press the issue a bit further, however, and the alignment begins to splinter. Under cross-examination regarding their *positive* commitments, beyond the various tactics of critique, psychoanalysis and existentialism both reveal in certain abiding assumptions regarding human autonomy the tenacious heritage of the Enlightenment. Moreover, they do this in different ways, so that they begin to criticize each other. The result is half exchange and half deadlock, a fair representation of how it stands with us at present in contemporary culture; and so we may wish to consider the matter more closely. Gerald Izenberg writes,

> In demonstrating that the ego was not master in its own house, psychoanalysis seemed to have struck the ultimate blow against rationalist optimism about the prospects of human freedom. Yet at the heart of Freud's interpretation of irrationality there were theoretical assumptions about the basic nature of human motivation and ideation which preserved in a priori form the idea of man's freedom and rationality, and thus created crucial gaps and inconsistencies in his explanations of clinical phenomena. Conversely, the existentialists were self-professedly militant proponents of the goal of authenticity in human life, of man's potential to be himself, to assume responsibility for his own possibilities and choices, and to live in accordance with this freedom rather than in subservience to the dictates of predetermined norms and roles. But the existential concept of authenticity has no positive content. The real substantive content of existentialism was a motivational theory of human *un*freedom that was more appropriate to the major clinical discoveries of Freud than some of his own metapsychological concepts and could be said to furnish their implicit theoretical underpinnings.[33]

Our rethinking of Freud via Lacan has been an effort to make good the gaps and inconsistencies to which Izenberg refers by way of something resembling the existentialist "theory of human unfreedom," as Izenberg requires. It remains to attempt, however briefly, the reciprocal task of considering existential authenticity in the light of psychoanalysis—and I think

---

[33] Ibid., pp. 3–4.

that we shall find, in so doing, that the effect is to create a dialogue between theology and psychoanalysis, through the medium of existentialism. For despite the decline in popularity of the explicitly existentialist literature, current theology remains enormously indebted to a variety of existentialist arguments and assumptions. One need only instance the common pattern in theology's dealings with psychoanalysis. Insofar as it coincides with existentialism, as for example in its dramatic view of the human condition, psychoanalysis has sometimes been endorsed; but insofar as it departs from a humanistic existentialism, as in its pessimistic view of human freedom, psychoanalysis has commonly been dismissed.

The effect of our own examination has been to relativize this existentialist imprimatur and thus to clear the way for psychoanalysis to reply. The heart of the response is to be found in the close interdependence of facticity and complicity. The existentialist tends to portray this relationship in ontological terms. By this very exaltation, separation is forced to sacrifice its specific character as an event, becoming instead a simple given; and the aura of fatalism thus introduced proceeds to suffuse the various forms of alienation, obscuring their psycho-social origins. It becomes hard to remember that *some* of the mute conditions which the ego confronts are its own handiwork returned to it—its sedimented history, as it were. These products of human doing, which Georg Lukács terms "second nature," get treated as if they were a cosmic bedrock.[34] The result is an open invitation to displace upon the cosmos the blame for our own institutionalized injustices. And as surely as the products of the ego are isolated and ontologized to the one side, the ego itself is isolated and ontologized to the other—this is the genesis of the phenomenon which Izenberg remarked, a notion of human freedom bereft of positive content.

To summarize: existentialism speaks the language of historicity yet its effect is to dehistoricize; psychoanalysis speaks the language of biology yet its effect is to render the human more radically historical. This somersaulting of the conventional wisdom is underlined by Russell Jacoby, who contends that "Freud's biologism is concentrated history while the historical consciousness of the post-Freudians is dressed-up biology. For the revisionists take what is the product of history and society—anxiety and insecurity—and translate it into a universal element of man's being—into biology. They gain existentialism and lose history."[35] This is the unacknowledged face of the exchange between existentialism and psychoanalysis, and it bears directly upon theology.

To make the bearing clear we need to take one further step. For if

---

[34] The pertinence of the concepts of "second nature" and "sedimented history," drawn from Hegel and Lukács, is argued by Russell Jacoby in *Social Amnesia*, pp. 31, 65; see also the Introduction and chapter 3 above.

[35] Ibid., p. 47.

psychoanalysis and existentialism concur on the tragic knot and part com-
pany over facticity and complicity, the payoff comes at the point of opposition. Anyone who has followed the rhetoric of existentialism can attest that
it thrives upon strong distinctions. Passion versus thought, qualitative versus
quantitative: whatever the content, sharp contrasts are required to get the
argument going. But Theodor Adorno wisely cautions that "in the history
of philosophy we repeatedly find epistemological categories turned into
moral ones"—and moral categories exalted above the ironies of history are
the makings of melodrama.[36] This penchant is most conspicuous in the case
of existentialism, but I believe that the same tendency may be observed in
theology and in the humanities more generally. Time and again what starts
out as an effort to give a balanced account of the human condition will
shift by imperceptible degrees into a *defense* of the *distinctively* human.[37]
When this happens, a price is paid in distortion, loss of context and a
softness on the side of melodrama. What is sacrificed is the balance Brown
envisioned, "a metaphysic which recognizes both *the continuity* between man
and the animals and also the discontinuity."

Imbalance is the price one pays for a polemical posture. The humanist,
we observed at the beginning of our discussion, has become preoccupied
with the task of refuting reductionism. This preoccupation lay behind the
common approach to psychology, namely the categorizing of good and bad
psychologies. And it lies behind the existentialist's denigration of the quantitative and the theoretical. Now in conclusion we can say why such
polemic must finally prove unfruitful. The reason, I believe, is that the
polemic bears more than a trace of what Lacan would call an Imaginary
opposition—the dynamics of a mimetic rivalry. It may well be that an
appropriate gloss on C. P. Snow's "two cultures" is Brown's remark that
"there are always two brothers . . . there are always two fraternities"—and
they are always in conflict.[38]

The test of this thesis would be to determine whether the humanist's
polemic exhibits the specific dynamic which distinguishes the Imaginary.
The Imaginary, we must remember, is not simply a matter of opposition; it
arises from a process of mirroring and thus it is a *dialectic* of opposition and

[36] Theodor W. Adorno, *Negative Dialectics* (New York: Seabury Press, 1973), p. 35. A related
caution is at least implicit within Peter Homans's *Theology after Freud*, which has been something of a landmark in the field. Much of the discussion there is directed against the notion
of a high and distant God, which Homans feels inevitably encourages the dynamics of psychic repression. But equally central is a critique of theological existentialism as being a "theology of the gaps"—one might say, a theology without mediations—and the aim of the
present essay has been, in effect, to expand on this latter theme.

[37] See Peter Homans, *Theology after Freud* (Indianapolis: Bobbs-Merrill, 1970), pp. 52ff.

[38] Brown, *Love's Body*, p. 22. Cf. Ricoeur's telling criticism of H. G. Gadamer's tendency
toward a romanticist dualism, in Ricoeur, "Philosophical Hermeneutics and Theological
Hermeneutics." Gadamer's assumptions in this connection are widely shared.

identification. Thus, the question would be whether theology, for example, in its anxiousness to stake out a turf of its own, might not have backed into an inadvertent mimicking of that which it would oppose. "Does science base itself upon the immediate data of the senses? Very well then, theology bases itself upon the immediate data of revelation." Reasoning such as this is not confined to the more fundamentalist sort of theology; it may equally well appear as an appeal to a self-authenticating I-Thou encounter. Or it may be expressed as a search for a 'good' psychology which might provide the theologian with a secure base or confirmation. In each case what is represented, I believe, is an alienated self-understanding, a forgetfulness of the insecurity which is inherent in the theological venture.[39]

The aim of this essay has been to recapture something of Freud's view of the human condition. I am aware that some will find the insistence upon tragedy too bleakly pessimistic while others will consider the suggestion of a Freudian eschatology a utopian fantasy. It is enough if I have succeeded in suggesting that the common criticisms of Freud miss much of what he has to say; and that one evidence of Freud's abiding relevance is his pressing upon the disciplines which had dismissed him the necessity of a radical self-critique—the necessity of rooting out the dynamics of Imaginary opposition.

At the same time it would be inappropriate for the last word to be defined by psychology, even if that word were a concept of tragedy or the necessity of self-critique. One does well to bear in mind Adorno's warning that the question with which we began, the question of the human condition, may be inherently ideological, "because its pure form dictates the invariant of the possible answer, even if that invariant is historicity itself."[40] In the last analysis, as it were, the outcome of theology's encounter with Freud may be measured in much the same way as the outcome of therapy. It is measured by the extent to which theology is enabled to speak in its own voice, delivered from the need for theological melodrama and restored to the world of difference and variance. It is measured by the extent to which theology is able to assume the language of tragedy and historicity not as an answer, but as a task.

---

[39] The background to these remarks is the critique of "identity theory" by the Frankfurt School of critical theory: e.g. by Adorno in *Negative Dialectics*, pp. 4–6 and in "Subject and Object," in *The Essential Frankfurt School Reader,* ed. A. Arato and F. Gebhardt (New York: Urizen Books, 1978). Significantly, Adorno's own aim is a certain recovery of "difference" (see *Negative Dialectics*, pp. 6, 13).

[40] Adorno, *Negative Dialectics*, p. 51.

CHAPTER FIVE
INNOCENCE AND EXPERIENCE

When the stars threw down their spears,
And water'd heaven with their tears,
Did he smile his work to see?
Did he who made the Lamb make thee?
William Blake
from "The Tyger"

Our responses to evil are almost always piecemeal and never, perhaps, consistent. One deals with such matters from moment to moment; and one lives, as it seems the human lot to live, between hope and desperation. In our own time, however, this common ambivalence has taken historical form. We inherit the optimism of the Enlightenment even as we inhabit the catastrophes of the twentieth century. Little wonder then that at one moment folk seem prepared to hypostatize evil, to regard it as an independent and alien power (witness the current fascination with the demonic) while the next moment they speak of occasions of suffering as being somehow a good, "a learning experience." The first effort of this essay will be to bring clarity to these mingled intuitions: to sort out the "modern" and "postmodern" viewpoints and arrange them as a successive debate, a genealogy of our present ambivalence.

This attempted, I then wish to focus on a certain notion of "integration" which presents itself, in psychology and in theology, as a way of recognizing this ambivalence and overcoming it. The clearest example of this proposal is C. G. Jung, who argues forcefully that evil is indeed a reality, but that by an appropriate confrontation with evil one can grow to greater individuation. Thus the phenomenon of evil is integrated into a complex notion of growth. But the integrative proposal has significance extending beyond the psychology of Jung; it is informed by a sense that all life is born of struggle, an intuition which many thinkers, among them the theologian Paul Tillich, have found to be deeply compelling. It is important therefore to clarify this integrative proposal as a way of responding to the problem of evil, and to determine to what degree it is successful. The second half of the essay attempts to do this. I shall argue that what gives the proposal its compelling character, in spite of certain manifest inconsistencies, is the fact that it embodies a powerful set of unresolved issues which we inherit from our religious and cultural past. To help define these issues, which are foreshadowed in the passage from Blake, the essay will make one more historical move, pressing back from the Jung-Tillich position to its roots in German idealism.

Finally, a concluding section will offer some theological proposals. In a much-quoted dictum, Tillich suggests that each age has its distinctive question. In the time of early Christianity it was the question of life in the face of death; in the time of the Reformation, the question of justification in the face of sin; and in the contemporary world, the question of meaning in the face of absurdity.[1] In this anguished interrogation Tillich gives a virtual epidemiology of the problem of evil, the various ways it has been experienced. Our own typology will indicate something similar. But for Tillich the primary use of the typology is as a guide to theological relevance, to help one identify the question of the day so that one may then address it. So used, it tends to assume the current question and not to look behind it. It fails to ask, for example, just what was involved in the shift away from the question of sin: what was gained, what was lost, what were the conscious and unconscious motivations? Questions such as these I hope at least to adumbrate, in the conviction that our given preoccupations must be respected, but also examined and "deconstructed." In that critical effort I will seek direction from a certain concept of "innocence."

1. Some terms of the discussion

Theology has long distinguished between "moral" and "natural" evil. Moral evil is identified by the fact that it requires some human agency. The child abuse which tormented Ivan in *The Brothers Karamazov* was a moral evil: somebody was responsible. In contrast the Lisbon earthquake which posed such questions for Voltaire was an instance of natural evil. The problem was precisely that no person or persons—lest it be God—could be held accountable.

If theology provides the distinction, psychoanalysis shows how profoundly the two factors intertwine. The impact of the study of the unconscious in this regard is a bit like what has happened to our understanding of cancer. Not long ago cancer was taken to be the classic example of natural evil. The disease was devastating and arbitrary in its occurrence; it bore no apparent relation to human agency. But as we have come to recognize the role of environmental factors arising from human action and neglect, the picture has become more complex. Analogously with psychoanalysis: it has led to deeper and deeper levels of interplay between nature and nurture, what is given and what is chosen; and thus, when one speaks of suffering, between natural and moral evil. For example, a suffering which had seemed accidental might emerge through analysis as a punishment one had inflicted

---

[1] Paul Tillich, *The Courage to Be* (New Haven: Yale University Press, 1952), pp. 40–63.

upon oneself. What had seemed a natural evil turns out to be a special case of moral evil, the result of unconscious intent. But then one's reflection may take a further turn: for are we really morally responsible for our unconscious motivations? Of course they are in some sense our own, but they are also the result of a larger situation. The Oedipal dilemma, for example, is not simply our own contrivance nor that of society at large. To some extent, which is no less important for being hard to define, it reflects the human condition. And so moral evil returns one to natural evil—to certain ineluctable realities which are not of human choosing.

In this manner psychoanalysis opens new levels of understanding and compassion. And yet, ironically, this very sophistication may lead to simplifications of its own. For, tracing back the interrelated factors in various lives, one returns time and again to a few irreducible constants. The story seems always the same, and so one may despair that anything can really be changed. Newly sensitized to the power of circumstance, to the pervasiveness of natural evil, one sees how the harshness of life enters into the very constitution of the self. And understanding all, one forgives all; one holds no one responsible. Collective absolution is achieved, but at the price of a fatalism which surrenders any notion of human freedom. Or alternatively the simplification may be launched from the side of the optimist. Consider the upbeat maxim that "your life is what you make of it." It may come as a liberating word when spoken in the proper context; but taken as a key to life, it self-destructs. As Philip Slater reminds us, "the core fallacy of the idea of progress is the notion that it is possible to optimize everything at once. This is a cherished liberal illusion in America, and its collapse leads naturally to apocalyptic visions."[2] And behind the imagery of annihilation there may lie a suppressed anger at oneself; for in a world which one has imagined to be without limits, there is only oneself to blame.

But if the former simplification denies moral evil just as the latter does natural evil, it is because both positions are implicitly bent upon *overcoming* evil altogether. If our lives are what we make of them, then a perfect existence is within our grasp and evil may be conquered. And if one believes, alternatively, that all that happens is more or less inevitable, then that too is a sort of solution. The fatalist has the security of believing that it is simply naive to complain or to call something evil; one can only say resignedly, "so it goes."

In such efforts at forced resolution, the issue is not encountered but deflected, not truly answered but dissolved. Perhaps one should say that it is repressed. And yet in candor we may have to acknowledge that by their very ambivalence, these simplifications are representative. For with all of us, perhaps, the problem of evil takes the form of an insistent, repressed awareness. That is to say, it is a pressing preoccupation which may assert itself in

[2] Philip Slater, *Earthwalk* (Garden City, NY: Anchor Press, Doubleday, 1974).

unintended ways and yet prove resistant to conscious articulation. Thus we
return from another angle to the ambivalence we noted at the outset. But
now it is apparent that the ambivalence can affect the problem itself, giving
it a peculiarly elusive character. The problem exists in a state of suspension
between being recognized and being dissolved. It is the soul-wrenching cry
of humankind—and yet it proves strangely evanescent.

It follows, then, that a dialogue between psychoanalysis and theology cannot simply be a matter of seeking to respond to the problem of evil. It must
include the task of *preserving* the problem, as well—allowing its full dimensions to emerge and fending off hasty solutions. The latter task requires a sort
of therapeutic alertness to the perils of premature cloture; and it also requires a
theological awareness of the ways in which, historically, the crucial categories
of moral and natural evil have variously been collapsed.

2. Traditional response / modern critique

Theology itself is not the place to start if one wishes to understand a
religious tradition. One should attend to the first-order language of worship,
the language addressed *to* God, before proceeding to theology, which is
second-order reflection *about* God. Approaching ancient Israel through its
worship one finds that the community was far from ignoring the reality of
suffering.

> See, Lord, how sorely I am distressed.
> > My bowels writhe in anguish
> and my stomach turns within me,
> > because I wantonly rebelled.
> The sword makes orphans in the streets,
> > as plague does within doors.   (Lamentations 1:20)

Moral evil outside the doors, natural evil within. And to this implicit distinction the passage adds another of equal importance: lamentation over the evil
one suffers and confession of evil committed. The act of confession is a distinguishing trait of the religious traditions. It has the effect of transforming the
general notion of moral evil into the specific notion of sin. "For I know my
transgressions, and my sin is ever before me. Against thee, thee only, have I
sinned, and done that which is evil in thy sight." (Psalm 51:3-4). This suggests
a sort of solution to the problem of evil: suffering may be regarded as punishment for sin. But at the same time it raises questions of its own, for the act of
confession, as the philosopher Paul Ricoeur has shown, is never self-
explanatory. It always has something of the character of a leap, and it is
rooted in a complex symbology.[3]

---

[3] Paul Ricoeur, *The Symbolism of Evil*, trans. Emerson Buchanan (New York: Harper and
Row, 1967), pp. 347-57.

What is crucial, in any event, is that in speaking the words of lamentation and confession—and in addressing them to a God who, by the very fact of being so addressed, is presumed powerful and good—the community locates itself at the heart of some powerful tensions. There is tension between the community's sin and God's righteousness, and tension between the community's actual suffering and the gracious power of God. Theology, as the language of religious reflection, is simply one way of dealing with these tensions. In examining how theology attempts to do this, I wish to focus on one historical strand or formulation. It is somewhat specific to Christianity and is far from exhausting even that tradition, but it has been of immeasurable influence throughout the history of the West, and so in any discussion of the problem of evil it merits examination.[4]

St. Augustine is the natural representative of this theology; he articulated it most forcefully and he stands as a watershed in its history.[5] The line of thought traces back to Plotinus and thence to Plato, and it proceeds forward through Thomas Aquinas and thence into modern theology, both Catholic and Protestant. It is "realist" in the sense that it regarded the Good as a reality and not simply an abstract ideal. Indeed the epochal significance of this theology was that it brought Being and the Good into the closest proximity; they were virtually identified. But, as Plato says of God in the *Timaeus*,

> He was good, and the good can never have any jealousy of anything. And being free from jealousy, he desired that all things should be as like himself as they could be. This is in the truest sense the origin of creation and of the world. . . .[6]

Thus, as the historian Arthur O. Lovejoy observes, "the concept of Self-Sufficing Perfection, by a bold logical inversion, was—without losing any of its original implications—converted into the concept of a Self-Transcending Fecundity."[7] The Good was conceived as *plenitude*, like the fullness of light which produces the spectrum of colors, or like a great, incessant fountain which leaps, splashes and spreads its abundance throughout the garden below. Evil, in such a context, cannot be a rival being. It must be regarded as an absence of the good abundance, as a debility or a lack. Correlative to the principle of plenitude, therefore, is this conception of evil as *privatio boni*, the privation of good.

This is not to say that evil is mere illusion. The absence of food is, for

[4] My exposition is distinctly indebted to John Hick's *Evil and the God of Love* (New York: Harper and Row, 1966), though it departs from Hick at some crucial points.

[5] Hick, *Evil and the God of Love*, p. 43.

[6] Plato, *Timaeus* (trans. B. Jowett), 29–30.

[7] Arthur O. Lovejoy, *The Great Chain of Being: A Study of the History of an Idea* (New York: Harper Torchbooks, 1936), p. 49.

the hungry, all too real. But it is to say that the reality of evil is precisely the reality of an absence: a violence to the fullness of things. Evil, like blindness, is parasitic upon a good. Now the virtue of this position, indeed its healing power, is in rescuing us from a view of the world which is profoundly unintegrated or dualistic, a view in which reality is ultimately divided between the powers of good and evil. Thus the concepts of plenitude and privation taken together may go a long way toward reconciling the tension noted earlier between the suffering of the creature and the goodness of the Creator. Certainly Augustine, for his part, experienced a providential fit between this aspect of Neoplatonism and the Christian view of creation.[8] Augustine is now able to argue that God does not in fact create evil, but simply creates a universe with certain lacks and limitations. There is limitation in the very fact of being a creature and not another god, and limitation too in being material. And limitations of this sort account for much of what we call evil. For in a finite, material world things collide and cause each other injury. The cancer cell, in thriving, preempts another's space.

But if collisions will inevitably happen, why create such a world at all? Here the principle of plenitude comes into play. The theologian Austin Farrer, following Augustine, offers an allegorical illustration. Imagine, if you will, a gardener who has filled all the beds within his plot:

> These having been created, a fresh choice has to be made. All the possibility of spiritual nature has been realized—everything you could call garden soil has been brought under cultivation. Only dry walls and rocks remain. What can the gardener do with stones? He can slip little plants into the crannies; and he may reckon it the furthest stretch of his art, to have made such barrenness bloom. So, beyond the spiritual there lies the possibility of the material. The creator does not hold his hand. It is better a physical universe, with its inevitable flaws, should be, than not be; and from the stony soil of matter he raises first living, and then reasonable creatures.[9]

With the appearance of these "reasonable creatures" we are at a further crossroads. The human is a fallible being; a certain frailty inheres in the limitations of being this particular kind of creature. Thus, in effect, natural evil provides moral evil with a foothold in the created order. But sin, the failure of this particular creature, is not simply one more mishap among others. It is, for Augustine and for the Christian tradition generally, rebellion—the perverse and willful severance of the personal, covenantal relationship which hitherto existed between creature and Creator. The covenant, then, is the necessary context; as Ricoeur observes, "it is in the

---

[8] Hick, *Evil and the God of Love*, p. 175.
[9] Austin Farrer, *Love Almighty and Ills Unlimited* (London: Fontana, 1962), pp. 65–66.

exchange between vocation and invocation that the whole experience of sin is found."[10] This is the reason that, as noted earlier, the confession of sin is not self-explanatory. Thus for Augustine the severity of the consequence—expulsion from Eden into a world of labor and pain—is but the measure of the good that was lost. It follows that while natural evil does provide a partial precondition for moral evil, sin itself impacts upon the natural order; consequences radiate out from the initial human act, until they return upon us in the form of a distorted, fallen creation.

To the modern mind instructed by the Enlightenment, the Christian story of paradise lost is altogether implausible and too sweepingly pessimistic. Most objectionable of all, perhaps, is the fact that such talk of sin and evil promotes a fatalism of the human spirit, reinforcing entrenched powers of reaction and oppression. In the face of such intransigence, the Enlightenment affirmed what might be called the discovery of human autonomy. Political autonomy in the form of democracy, scientific autonomy in the form of independent investigation—these spring from a brave refusal to believe there is a fundamental flaw at the heart of things. The conviction of hope, more than any issue of historical plausibility, accounts for the modern dismissal of the Augustinian formulation. And this venerable construction of the debate—Augustine to the one side, the Enlightenment to the other—continues to the present day in many of the various disputes between theology and psychology.

3. Modern response / postmodern critique

But for all its fervent iconoclasm, the remarkable fact about the Enlightenment is that it actually carried forward—in secularized form—the same, essential structures of the Augustinian formulation. Indeed one might argue that in this period the structures are not only continued but reinforced. For in Augustine there were counterbalances; the second-order concepts of plenitude and privation had to coexist with a mythic-symbolic heritage which often pointed in other directions. The Enlightenment was, in contrast, single-mindedly rational; in that atmosphere the concepts of plenitude and privation, released of their former symbolic ballast, became increasingly expansive and rarefied.

Evidence of the continuance of this concept of plenitude is found in Lovejoy's seminal study, *The Great Chain of Being*. (Indeed the "principle of plenitude" is Lovejoy's phrase.) The translation of plenitude into secular terms was accomplished by a hierarchical view of Nature in which Nature tended to become in Crane Brinton's words "a hypostatized conception of the beautiful and the good."[11] The way in which the period used this comforting notion

[10] Ricoeur, *Symbolism of Evil*, p. 52.
[11] Crane Brinton, "Enlightenment," in *The Encyclopedia of Philosophy*, ed. Paul Edwards (New York: Macmillan, 1967), 1:520.

was not so naive as is sometimes alleged. Leibniz could speak of "the best of all possible worlds," but his intention was less to claim perfection for this world than to expose the deficiencies of the alternatives. Still when all is said and done the temper of the times was decidedly upbeat; and for this fresh spirit of hope, the notion of a plenitudinous Nature provided a benevolent endorsement.

The full reach of Enlightenment aspiration is attested by the notion of Progress and the brave endeavors it underwrote. In this concept one encounters the unswerving advocacy of a secularized *privatio boni*. On this view evil is not a hostile power, nor even a permanent warp in the given nature of things. Natural evil is reduced to a passing aberration, a deflection from natural order. And humankind, who is to put matters right, is hampered in that effort by nothing more serious than ignorance and superstition, the Enlightenment translation of sin.

This brief account is perhaps too critical, too little appreciative of the magnificent achievements to which hopefulness gave birth. But who today can write of the Enlightenment without an acute awareness that the convictions which were so intensified in the eighteenth century collapsed in the twentieth? Total warfare—as reality and as image—has invaded the furthest recess of this century's experience, dispelling forever that confident faith in the human prospect. On these grounds I wish to distinguish the "modern" and "postmodern" worldviews, taking psychoanalysis and existentialism as representative of the later period. In the previous chapter we saw how these two movements are at one in extending the range of the problem of evil. For neither of them is natural evil confined to physical nature; for neither is it a remediable problem, a mere puzzle to be solved. Instead natural evil is radicalized; it becomes a "tragic knot" in the very nature of things, by virtue of which the promotion of one value and the destruction of another are tragically intertwined. In Freud this condition is represented by the interdependence of Eros and Thanatos; in Sartre it is seen in the human alliance with Nothingness.[12] The dilemmas which result are fundamentally irresolvable. Such good as is achieved is won at a sobering price. Humanity is no longer the proud exception, the privileged solution to the cosmic flaw. Entirely the contrary, the emergence of the human serves only to reestablish the cosmic travail in another, more intense form. So far from being a resolution, humanity is for Eros and Thanatos, or Being and Nothingness, the locus of ultimate collision.

The imagery of collision is not accidental. Psychoanalysis and existentialism, however much they be revised, are conflictual views of the human

---

[12] For the sake of simplicity the present discussion is confined to the early Sartre of *Being and Nothingness*. In formulating the terms of the Freud-Jung contrast the typology is indebted to the work of Philip Rieff, *The Triumph of the Therapeutic: Uses of Faith after Freud* (New York: Harper Torchbooks, 1966).

condition. One might argue against them that for just this reason they mirror too much the strife-torn age they would critique. But it is the achievement of all great movements to embody the contradictions of their time; and in any event, whatever hope is to be found in the twentieth century is the hope of touching bottom, finding in the hardest truth firm ground on which to stand. This difficult message achieves a sort of popular recognition in the picture of Freud as one who dealt in sinister forces. Such notions of the unconscious are no doubt simplistic; but they reflect a valid intuition that life is more difficult than the Enlightenment thought, and that when the bright demigods of Enlightenment recede, the chthonic powers emerge. Inchoate dualism is the price we pay for the loss of the *privatio.*

Stepping back for a moment now, we may appreciate the effect of the "modern/postmodern" distinction in converting the tired debate between religion and science, Augustine and the Enlightenment, into a more nuanced three-part discussion. It becomes imaginable that theology and psychoanalysis might strike an alliance against the myopia of the earlier age.

> He eats the droppings from his own table; thus he manages to stuff himself fuller than the others for a little, but meanwhile he forgets how to eat from the table; thus in time even the droppings cease to fall.[13]

Could Kafka be speaking of the Enlightenment mind, which inherited the traditional concepts and even expanded their domain, but failed to give them the needed rootage? Certainly Reinhold Niebuhr, Paul Tillich, Richard Rubenstein and other theologians have challenged "the easy conscience of modern man" by drawing upon the critical insights of existentialism and psychoanalysis.[14] Thus a shared commitment to critical realism suggests that theology and psychoanalysis might provisionally become allied not in spite of, but precisely because of, the abiding problem of evil.

4. Postmodern analytic response / postmodern integrative critique

The postmodern period itself, however, is not a uniform phenomenon. The historian Gerald N. Izenberg lays the foundations for an important distinction in his study on *The Existentialist Critique of Freud.* In a manner consonant with our own account, Izenberg portrays psychoanalysis and existentialism as precipitating a "crisis of autonomy," the collective dismantling

---

[13] *The Viking Book of Aphorisms,* ed. W. H. Auden and Louis Kronenberger (New York: Viking Press, 1962), p. 92; quoted without specific reference.
[14] Reinhold Niebuhr, *The Nature and Destiny of Man: A Christian Interpretation,* 2 vols. (New York: Scribners, 1941), 1:93; Paul Tillich, *Theology of Culture* (New York: Oxford University Press, 1959); Richard L. Rubenstein, *The Religious Imagination: A Study in Psychoanalysis and Jewish Theology* (Boston: Beacon Press, 1968).

of the Enlightenment confidence that the ego is master in its own house. But Izenberg goes on to show that, at the same time, each movement bore within itself a powerful *countercurrent* which pointed in a direction precisely contrary to that of the original critique. Thus as regards psychoanalysis: "at the heart of Freud's interpretation of irrationality there were theoretical assumptions about the basic nature of human motivation and ideation which preserved in a priori form the idea of man's freedom and rationality, and thus created crucial gaps and inconsistencies in his explanation of clinical phenomena." Similarly "the real substantive content of existentialism was a motivational theory" not of freedom but of "unfreedom"—yet the thrust of the movement was an insistent appeal to the individual's free and inescapable responsibility.[15]

Viewed in the abstract this coexistence of currents and countercurrents seems entirely paradoxical. Viewed historically, however, the anomalies appear quite natural; for just as elements of the Augustinian formulation survived into the modern period, so remnants of the modern could be expected to perdure into postmodernity. It is in this manner that Izenberg himself tends to regard the phenomenon. But our own thematic would suggest that the survival of these particular convictions is not simply an historical accident. For is it not apparent that having pressed to the extremes of estrangement, having laid bare the human plight, the movements themselves were in urgent need of a ground to stand on? Paradigmatic in this regard is the Freud of *The Future of an Illusion*, who, having diagnosed the various besiegements and ruses of human history, avows that a chastened faith in the insistence of reason is his own inexpungible "illusion."[16] He might have said, following Kant, that it is a sort of postulate of practical reason.

But the reference to Kant suggests what Jürgen Habermas has argued at length, that the concepts of "freedom" and "reason" in certain post-modern thinkers are not simply inherited but transformed.[17] For one thing, they are not so substantialized. As Sartre would have it, freedom pertains not to our essence but our existence; and reason in Freud is no longer Reason, no longer the mirror of an abiding Nature which is itself "a hypostatized conception of the beautiful and the good." But the transformation goes further; for freedom and reason, having surrendered their separate and self-evident moorings, become radically interdependent. This is one implication

[15] Gerald N. Izenberg, *The Existentialist Critique of Freud: The Crisis of Autonomy* (Princeton: Princeton University Press, 1976), pp. 3–4.

[16] Sigmund Freud, "The Future of an Illusion," in *The Standard Edition of the Complete Psychological Works of Sigmund Freud*, trans. under the general editorship of James Strachey, 24 vols. (London: Hogarth Press, 1961), 21:53.

[17] Jürgen Habermas, *Knowledge and Human Interests*, trans. Jeremy J. Shapiro (Boston: Beacon Press, 1971), p. 214.

of Habermas's notion of an "emancipatory cognitive interest."[18] Reason becomes a function of freedom, no longer a given but a human project. And freedom becomes the goal of reason, for reason is now understood as stringently reflective and analytic; its task is to critique, to unmask, and thus to free from self-delusion. But such freedom is relative and of the moment: Sartre's critique of bad faith and Freud's analysis of neurosis are unsupported by utopian assurance. Thus there is about them, for all their occasional excesses, a certain tragic reserve—and that tragic stance is in its own right a sort of response to the problem of evil. It is not a cosmic solution, to be sure, but for Sartre and for Freud that is just the point. It is a way of living which is its own justification. Its good lies not in some eventual and hypothetical outcome, but simply in the fact that in and through its struggle for emancipation it is a way of being human.

To this postmodern analytic position I now wish to contrast an alternative position epitomized by C. G. Jung. The issue at stake is not the analytic per se, as all parties agree it is indispensable, but whether the analytic in and of itself can be *sufficient*.[19] Thus Jung begins with a qualified endorsement of the analytic: Freud was "a great destroyer" who dissolved forever the complacency of his age. "All that gush about man's innate goodness, which had addled so many brains after the dogma of original sin was no longer understood, was blown to the winds by Freud. . . ."[20] Jung wishes to set himself over against Enligtenment modernity, on the side of the postmodern and shoulder to shoulder with Freud. But Jung is emphatic that, however necessary the analytic may be, it must never presume to be sufficient. To establish this, Jung introduces a sharp distinction between the patient and the healthy individual. "With our patients 'analytical' understanding has a wholesomely destructive effect, like a corrosive or thermocautery, but it is banefully destructive on sound tissue." He can even say, "it is a technique we have learned from the devil. . . . The menacing and dangerous thing about analysis is that the individual is apparently understood: the devil eats his soul away. . . ."[21] The movement of analysis must be countered and completed by another more generous method which can offer vision to the seeker and hope to the sick.

Closely paralleling Jung's proposals regarding psychoanalysis are certain philosophic proposals which would revise and expand the Sartrean form of existentialism. For our purposes it will be useful to note the form this existential revisionism takes in the thought of Paul Tillich, and to observe particularly his criticism of Freud. Tillich grounds his position on "three

[18] Ibid., p. 310.

[19] Cf. Rieff, *Triumph of the Therapeutic*, p. 87.

[20] Carl G. Jung, *Collected Works* (Princeton: Princeton University Press, 1954-), 15:46.

[21] Carl G. Jung, *Letters*, ed. Gerhard Adler and Aniela Jaffe (Princeton: Princeton University Press, 1973), 1:31-32. Cf. Peter Homans, *Jung in Context: Modernity and the Making of Psychology* (Chicago: University of Chicago Press, 1979), p. 94.

considerations of human nature" which "are present in all genuine theological thinking." They are "essential goodness, existential estrangement, and
the possibility of something, a 'third,' beyond essence and existence, through
which the cleavage is overcome and healed."[22] Tillich's terminology should
become clearer in the course of the following section; the important thing
for the moment is its application to Freud. The schema enables Tillich to
applaud Freud regarding the second of the three points, his treatment of
"existential estrangement," while faulting him on the first and third. Like
Jung, Tillich endorses the Freudian realism. He portrays psychoanalysis as
voicing, along with existentialism, a much-needed protest against the "philosophies of consciousness" of the Enlightenment.[23] But Tillich regrets that
Freud confined himself to this critical task. Freud "does not know any other
man" than the figure of existential estrangement (though something more is
prefigured in Freud's own therapy); "and this is the basic criticism that
theology would weigh against him on this point."[24] Thus Tillich like Jung
seeks to relativize Freud within a larger framework: and what that framework adds, again as in Jung, is a notion of residual goodness and a vision of
reconciliation.

5. Postmodern integrative response

The three considerations Tillich finds so fundamental for theology move
from an initial untroubled unity, through alienation and conflict, to a final
reconciliation. In the course of Tillich's work this sequence appears and
reappears, shaping much of his theology. And in Jung, as is well known, a
similar sequence is equally fundamental. It is the process of individuation,
proceeding out of a primordial, unreflective one into an individualized existence in which reflective awareness is achieved, but at the price of confine-
ment to the ego; and thence to a final state in which the unconscious is
admitted, "the scope of consciousness is widened, and through the fact that the
paradoxes have been made conscious the sources of conflict are dried up."[25]

Thus there is a common "integrative" structure. But our typology has
to do specifically with responses to the problem of evil; we need to ask
therefore to what constructive *use* the structures are put. Here too the parallel seems to hold: both Tillich and Jung propose what one might call a
"postmodern recuperation." That is to say, they begin by affirming a postmodern analytic mode of thought, viz. classical existentialism in the one

[22] Tillich, *Theology of Culture*, p. 119.
[23] Ibid., p. 114. In this context Tillich is incidentally critical of Jung (ibid., p. 122). The
effect of the typology is to suggest that beyond such differences there are more fundamental,
structural affinities.
[24] Ibid., p. 120.
[25] Carl G. Jung, *Psychological Reflections*, ed. Jolande Jacobi (New York: Harper Torchbooks,
1953), p. 274.

case and Freudian psychoanalysis in the other; but then they seek to reach back behind the analytic to an earlier, religious coherence. This done, they further propose to bring that religious vision forward—reinterpreting in terms of modern autonomy, and further reinterpreting in terms of postmodern tragedy—until at last it can emerge into the present time as a relevant, healing word. In the process the integrative sequence serves as both solution and diagnosis. The distant past corresponds (historically and/or symbolically) to the state of primordial oneness, our present experience to the state of conflict, and beyond that we are offered the vision of reconciliation. But if this is so, if this is the purpose they have in mind, then do we not have in Jung and Tillich a further response to the problem of evil?

In Jung the answer is clear. In the state of conflict as Jung describes it we confront some other reality as alien, threatening—and evil. Individuation is conceived as a response to this problem; it means affirming that other as an estranged aspect of one's self. And in that final state of enrichment and resolution the conflict is taken up, overcome—and justified. With Tillich the answer is less clear; matters are complicated by his concern to square his use of the structure with the claims of the tradition. In order to treat these complexities, I shall concentrate on Tillich in the present section. This will also help us identify the theological issues which the integrative response implicitly raises. But it should be remembered all the while that the task is to think Tillich and Jung together as a type, with Jung presenting in its purity a structure of thought to which Tillich is deeply committed, but about which he remains ambivalent.

The first of Tillich's three moments is a condition of "dreaming innocence," an untroubled communion with the ground of Being or God. But it is a quasi-unconscious state, a suspended potentiality, and that is its limitation. Tillich suggests a psychological analogy:

> Up to a certain point, the child is unconscious of his sexual potentialities. In the difficult steps of transition from potentiality to actuality, an awakening takes place. Experience, responsibility, and guilt are acquired, and the state of dreaming innocence is lost. This example is evident in the biblical story, where sexual consciousness is the first consequence of the loss of innocence.[26]

Consciousness and guilt: this is the classic Tillichian "method of correlation." The Fall and original sin, those seemingly implausible Augustinian doctrines, are given new currency by being imaginatively related to deep levels of experience, the very emergence of consciousness. But in being brought forward in this fashion, the doctrines are inevitably reinterpreted. The Fall is no longer a past event, but an abiding truth of the human condition. The

[26] Paul Tillich, *Systematic Theology*, 3 vols. (Chicago: University of Chicago Press, 1951–1963), 2:34.

biblical story becomes a way of naming our present experience. It names the modern discovery of human autonomy as a sort of awakening; and it illumines the postmodern experience that the assertion of autonomy has left in its wake a seemingly inescapable guilt.

Seemingly inescapable indeed. The question which has to be asked is whether Tillich, in the course of his brilliant interpretation, has not linked consciousness and guilt so closely that guilt becomes a part of our given condition. In that case guilt shifts from the realm of the moral to that of the natural—and then what sense could there be in calling it guilt? Tillich addresses this question by making a crucial distinction with regard to the second or conflictual moment of his three-part schema. It is the distinction between existence and estrangement. "*Existence*," as Tillich is fond of noting, derives from a Latin root meaning "to stand out."[27] In moving from potentiality to actuality, a being must stand out; that is to say, it must separate itself from, or attenuate its participation in, the supportive ground of its Being. In the terms of Tillich's psychological analogy, the child must leave its mother.[28] This much is necessary and natural. But *estrangement* is another matter: it means being not simply distinct, autonomous, but in opposition. It suggests a radical rebellion and refusal which Tillich, following the tradition, calls sin. Sin is alienation from God, or in Tillich's language alienation from the ground of Being.

The question thus comes down to the relation between existence and estrangement. Tillich tells us our existence is estranged. But did it *have* to be? Tillich disavows any logical necessity but then goes on to say that nevertheless in point of fact, "actualized creation and estranged existence are identical": there is a "coincidence of creation and the Fall."[29] This is where Tillich's critics become restive. They charge that Tillich has made sin a necessary part of the created order, impugning the goodness of the Creator.[30] For what sort of God would it be who condemned us for doing what we could not help, for being as God had made us? But Tillich denies this inference; he holds that it is we who are responsible. For remember that estrangement is still contingent upon the act of freedom; "the child, upon growing into maturity, affirms the state of estrangement in acts of freedom which imply responsibility and guilt."[31] But the critics are quick to note that Tillich is not talking about making a bad choice in lieu of a good one,

---

[27] Ibid., p. 20.

[28] G. B. Hammond, *The Power of Self-Transcendence: An Introduction to the Philosophical Theology of Paul Tillich* (St. Louis: Bethany, 1966), p. 64.

[29] Tillich, *Systematic Theology*, 2:44.

[30] E.g. Reinhold Niebuhr, "Biblical Thought and Ontological Speculation in Tillich's Theology," in *The Theology of Paul Tillich*, ed. C. W. Kegley and R. W. Bretall (New York: Macmillan, 1952), pp. 220–27; K. Hamilton, *The System and the Gospel: A Critique of Paul Tillich* (New York: Macmillan, 1963), pp. 147–57.

[31] Tillich, *Systematic Theology*, 2:44.

choosing the apple rather than another fruit, but making *any* choice at all. The only alternative would be to remain in sheer potentiality, which is probably impossible and in any case scarcely honorable. Yet for Tillich that dilemma is precisely the point: we are in fact forced to choose between a vacuous innocence and a guilty autonomy. And if this seems objectionable, if the notion of guilt seems oddly situated here, Tillich's response in effect is, "Don't blame me. Blame experience, blame life, blame the Scriptures!"

What I have presented here is a stylized synopsis of a complex debate, a disputed question in recent theology. It may suffice to give one a sense of the unresolved issues which hover about the integrative proposal. As for the definition of Tillich's own position, we may place some confidence in the findings of Joel R. Smith, who has pursued the issue of estrangement through a number of Tillichian texts. Smith concludes that there is indeed an ambiguity in Tillich's handling of the matter, traceable to a "background tendency" which Smith describes as a "quasi-Hegelian dialectic in which actualization occurs through a process of estrangement which culminates in reconciliation."[32] Let us reserve Hegel for the moment; what Jones is saying, translated into our own terminology, is that the ambiguity arises from Tillich's effort to wed the threepart integrative schema with the traditional Christian doctrines. But if this is so, we have to ask what there is about this schema to make it so compelling that Tillich the systematician was determined to retain it, even at the price of such conceptual dissonance.

To answer this question I suggest we shift our attention from the time-worn issue of how existence and estrangement are related, to the issue of how each is to be *assessed*. What value or disvalue does each of these concepts convey? If we start with the concept of "existence" and try to imagine it in its own right, apart from estrangement, it is clearly a positive good. It is growth, actualization, the realization of latent potential. And if then we turn to "estrangement," it would seem correspondingly negative; for it is through estrangement that the structure of finitude is transformed into "a structure of destruction."[33] But perhaps this negative judgment is too hasty; perhaps it takes too narrow a view. One must consider that in the total sweep of Tillich's theology "essential as well as existential elements are always abstractions from the concrete actuality of being, namely, 'Life.'" This notion of Life corresponds to the third of Tillich's moments or dimensions. And of the Divine Life Tillich writes,

> It is the nature of blessedness itself that requires a negative element in the eternity of the Divine Life.

---

[32] Joel R. Smith, "Creation, Fall and Theodicy in Paul Tillich's Systematic Theology," in *Kairos and Logos: Studies in the Roots and Implications of Tillich's Theology*, ed. J. J. Carey (Cambridge, MA: North American Paul Tillich Society, 1978), p. 183.

[33] Tillich, *Systematic Theology*, 2:71.

> This leads to the fundamental assertion: The Divine Life is the eternal conquest of the negative; this is its blessedness. Eternal blessedness is not a state of immovable perfection. . . . But the Divine Life is blessedness through fight and victory.[34]

In this statement we have, I believe, the fundamental reason so many folk sense in Tillich's account of sin a certain necessity. Whatever may be said about whether estrangement had to happen existentially, the crucial fact is that it had to happen in the *logic* of Tillich's theology, because the very system of that theology requires it. That is to say, Tillich's most basic framework requires that estrangement, which appears at close range to be entirely negative, should become in the larger scheme of things—and precisely because it is in the first instance so sheerly negative—a positive good. More exactly, it becomes part of a larger good, part of the Divine Life. As we have seen, Tillich says with disarming candor that the Divine Life "requires a negative element." Thus all that we might wish to call negative—be it evil, sin, estrangement—becomes in the larger picture a good! And that larger picture *is* the integrative schema. Now at last we can see what makes the schema so difficult and implausible, and yet so indispensable, so compelling. For in Tillich's use of it the schema becomes far more than a convenient way of organizing traditional Christian doctrine. It becomes in and of itself a distinctive theodicy, a response to the problem of evil.

And what Tillich suggests, Jung openly espouses. One passage merits quoting at length because it contains everything: the translation by way of the psychological analogy, the apparently negative but finally positive second moment, the vision of harmony:

> It is not without justification that the biblical story of creation put the undivided harmony of plant, animal, man, and God into the symbol of Paradise at the beginning of all psychic being, and described the first act of becoming conscious—"ye shall be as gods, knowing good and evil"—as the fatal sin. For it must appear as a sin to the naive mind to break the law of the sacred primordial oneness of all-consciousness. It is a luciferian defiance of the individual against the oneness. It is a hostile act of disharmony against harmony, it is separation over against all-embracing unity. And yet the gaining of consciousness was the most precious fruit on the tree of life, and the magic weapon which gave man mastery over the earth,

---

[34] Ibid., 3:405. Karl Barth was aware of how much rode on this seemingly subtle theological point. In sharp contrast to Tillich's proposal, see Barth's emphatic declaration that "reconciliation is anything but a synthesis of creation and covenant on the one hand and sin on the other. Between these there is no higher third thing in which they can be peacefully united. And reconciliation is not a higher unity. . . . Speculators of every kind are therefore warned." Karl Barth, *Church Dogmatics*, trans. G. W. Bromiley (Edinburgh: T & T Clark, 1956), 4/1:80.

and which we hope will enable him to win the even greater victory of mastery over himself.[35]

6. The idealist background

I now wish to pursue Smith's reference to "a quasi-Hegelian dialectic," for I do not believe that one can understand the integrative position, much less criticize it, without having considered its origins. Hegel himself, it should be said, would disavow the quasi-Hegelian, if by that is meant a simplistic cosmic foxtrot of thesis, antithesis and synthesis. The true point of lineage is rather that Hegel, and German idealism more generally, perfected an understanding of emergent self-consciousness very similar to what we have seen in Jung and Tillich. Further, we have just observed how the integrative position introduces what is in effect a revised notion of plenitude; and historically the great proponents of a revised form of plenitude have been, in the period since the Enlightenment, the idealists. Finally there is specific evidence that such parallels are not accidental. Jung and Tillich borrowed freely from a variety of figures in idealism, in the romanticism which is closely allied and in the earlier mysticism from which the idealists themselves drew inspiration.[36]

So just as thinking Jung and Tillich together helped us describe the integrative position, thinking the integrative in juxtaposition with idealism may help us assess it. This will require a bit of historical backtracking, however, in order to fill a gap in our earlier account; for while the Enlightenment was a phenomenon of the eighteenth century and postmodernism of the twentieth, idealism flowered in the century between. But the omission itself is significant. For our task has been to sort out the contemporary viewpoints on evil in light of their acknowledged sources and in much theological and psychological discussion, particularly in the United States, the role of idealism, while altogether crucial, has been largely unacknowledged. This point is argued in our third chapter; here it must suffice to suggest that we may be dealing with an instance of what the literary critic Harold Bloom has called "the anxiety of influence," a sort of Oedipal repression of an intellectual debt which remains unacknowledged because unresolved.[37]

Now the idealists themselves were at grips with St. Augustine, so we need to begin with him. Let us recall the mixed character of his treatment of evil. On the one hand he traced it to a variety of limitations and frailties

---

35 Jung, *Collected Works*, 10:139-40. See Howard L. Philip, *Jung and the Problem of Evil* (New York: R. M. McBride, 1958) and David B. Burrell, G. S. C., *Exercises in Religious Understanding* (Notre Dame: University of Notre Dame Press, 1974), pp. 217-32.

36 See J. A. Stone, "Tillich and Schelling's Later Philosophy," in *Kairos and Logos: Studies in the Roots and Implications of Tillich's Theology*, ed. J. J. Carey (Cambridge, MA: North American Paul Tillich Society, 1978).

37 Harold Bloom, *The Anxiety of Influence: A Theory of Poetry* (New York: Oxford University Press, 1973).

which were built into the created order. To this extent he implied that the
first evil was natural evil. But alongside this source he juxtaposed another,
namely the sin of Adam, rebellion against God, the great act of moral evil.
And of the two, he came down much more heavily upon the latter. Indeed
he asserts in a particularly straightforward phrase that all the evil we know
in this life is "either sin or punishment for sin."[38] Here is a treatment of
evil as sweeping, in its own way, as the integrative proposal that all suffering may finally be positive. For Augustine the pain of childbirth and pain
of death are not simply a function of the hardness of life, but the just punishment of a rebellious humanity.[39]

Little effort is needed to imagine how this proposal sat with the idealists, the zealous champions of human autonomy. In their eyes Augustine
was offering them a shell game or, in more juridical terms, a bum rap. At
one moment Augustine acknowledges that the first source of evil was in the
creation itself. Tygers, to use Blake's image, were created carnivorous—and
humans were created fallible. But the next moment the entire blame is
thrust upon a hapless humankind. Moreover, the idealists had a strong
suspicion of what it was that the Augustinian two-step was endeavoring to
hide. For it is clear that on a more candid accounting a substantial portion
of the responsibility would necessarily revert to God the Creator. Here is
Oedipal conflict of a high order indeed: the idealists were at grips not simply with Augustine, but with Augustine's God. This God appeared to them
as a vindictive Father who restricted his children's freedom and punished
the least infraction while yet disavowing his own inherent responsibility.
The reverberations of the idealists' struggle with this figure are with us still,
and not least in the broad cultural movement which came to public attention under the banner of "the death of God."

Those sensitive to the pathos and grandeur of this struggle, not to say
the simple justice of its cause, will have little time for the common carica-
ture of idealist philosophy as a frivolous mentalistic game. The struggle is
the birthright of idealism, a sort of coming-to-selfconsciousness of the modern age. And like many who engage the Oedipal process, the idealists
emerged from the struggle with a heightened sense of identity: an identity
which was distinctively their own and yet sought to be faithful to the
father's best principles—indeed more faithful than the father had been
himself. This effort is perhaps the key to idealism as a religious philosophy.
Certainly the God of the idealists is one who does not stand apart but is
profoundly involved in the struggles of this world, often to the point that
the creative wordly processes become but another face of divinity.

This brings us to the vision of final harmony which is the idealist's
future-oriented reappropriation of the principle of plenitude, and to the

---

[38] Augustine, *De Genesi Ad Litteram,* Imperfectus Liber, 1. 3.
[39] Hick, *Evil and the God of Love,* p. 65.

question of whether the proposal is persuasive. The debates on this question are classic, but the decisive issue is perhaps best captured by a well-known scene from *The Brothers Karamazov*. Ivan and Alyosha are alone in a room together. They have talked at length. Now Ivan addresses his brother with the utmost earnestness: "Listen! If all must suffer to pay for the eternal harmony, what have children to do with it, tell me, please? It's beyond all comprehension why they should suffer, and why they should pay for the harmony." And then:

> "Tell me yourself, I challenge you—answer. Imagine that you are creating a fabric of human destiny with the object of making men happy in the end, giving them peace and rest at last, but that it was essential and inevitable to torture to death only one tiny creature—that baby beating its breast with its fist, for instance—and to found that edifice on its unavenged tears, would you consent to be the architect on these conditions? Tell me, and tell me the truth."
> "No, I wouldn't consent," said Alyosha softly. . . .[40]

Let us be fair to idealism: it is not naively optimistic. The virtue of the path we have traced, approaching idealism through its continuity with postmodernity, has been to show that unlike the Enlightenment, the idealist position was not achieved by minimizing evil. Entirely to the contrary, the original thrust of idealism is precisely to confront the form of evil which Augustine implicitly discounted, namely the elements of suffering which are inherent in life itself. Yet when all is said and done there is in idealism the penchant toward final wholeness. The significance of this transcendent and enigmatic vision is that it impinges upon the present, extending consolation in the face of pain. And the logic of that consolation is to apprehend evil as something which, in its very negativity, contributes to a larger good. This is the background to Tillich's conviction that "the nature of blessedness itself . . . requires a negative element in the eternity of the Divine Life." Viewing the postmodern in light of this background, we see that the postmodern arises not only for historical reasons, because of the violence of the twentieth century, but for conceptual reasons as well, because of specific inadequacies in the Augustinian theology. And viewing the integrative proposal in this context, we see how it is that the proposal addresses the problem of evil with a special seriousness and yet is in danger of dissolving it.

Now the crucial theological assumption of this idealist-integrative position is, as Smith stresses, that "creation is fulfilled *by means of* rather than *in spite of* estrangement."[41] With this decisive question of whether creation is fulfilled by means of estrangement or in spite of it, we approach the headwaters of the

---

[40] Fyodor Dostoyevsky, *The Brothers Karamazov*, trans. Constance Garnett (New York: Modern Library, 1950), bk. 5: chap. 4.
[41] Smith, "Creation, Fall and Theodicy," p. 182.

problem of evil. Or to alter the metaphor, we find ourselves in the crosscurrents of two profoundly human and yet profoundly divergent intuitions. On the one hand, it is evident that one often grows through adversity. Who could possibly deny it? The spirit of our times is surely right in dismissing the cloistered virtue of those who hold life at arm's length. Life is in the struggle and tumble of things, and in the words of Goethe's *Faust*, "who strives always to the utmost, him can we save." But the idealist is committed to carrying to its fullest conclusion the modern discovery of human autonomy; indeed idealism is virtually defined by that determination; and therefore the idealist takes the axiom of growth-through-struggle and applies it to life in its *entirety*. The result is a revised principle of plenitude which understands all of experience in light of the growth toward which it tends. But we know that the earlier notion of plenitude came to seem impersonal and detached. What assurance is there now that the idealist proposal, however compassionate its intent, may not prove in the end to be equally inhumane? As Dostoyevsky is urgent to remind us, this eminently humanistic vision seems in practice to be of a piece with the chilling conclusion that the end justifies the means. Its ultimate logic seems to be that the end is achieved by means of, and not simply in spite of, the occurrence of innocent suffering.

But in even a single instance of innocent suffering there is that which resists this entire apparatus. It refuses to be reasoned or relativized or quantified in any way. As J. B. Metz insists, "The slightest trace of senseless suffering in the world of human experience gives the lie to all affirmative ontology and all teleology. . . ."[42] This recognition is in fact the second fundamental intuition, which Ivan's challenge sets before us. It is not necessarily self-evident. Why indeed should anyone be credited with being innocent? The very notion seems to share in the elusiveness of the problem of evil, of which it forms an inseparable part; and Ivan himself seems at times afraid that the anguished awareness may slip away. But for those who have eyes to see and ears to hear, the suffering of the innocent rebukes the friends of Job, who contend that none is truly innocent and all affliction is deserved. And it rebukes as well the friends' modern counterpart who speaks of a greater growth and resolution which will justify the suffering that went before. It is Metz's achievement to have pressed this point with lucidity; "no improvement of the condition of freedom in the world is able to do justice to the dead or effect a transformation of the injustice and the non-sense of past suffering."[43]

---

[42] Johann B. Metz, *Faith in History and Society: Toward a Practical Fundamental Theology*, trans. David Smith (New York: Seabury Press, 1980), p. 108. Metz cites Theodor Adorno's *Negative Dialectics*, trans. E. B. Ashton (New York: Seabury Press, 1973), in connection with this passage and again in connection with the passage quoted below.

[43] Metz, *Faith in History and Society*, p. 128.

Ivan faces us, then, with an inexorable choice. *Either* hold fast to the innocent suffering, hold fast to the *reality* of that "non-sense"—even if it means living without any larger context, without any vision of plenitude in which the suffering might come to make sense. *Or* surrender some part of the reality of that suffering, allow the memory to be somewhat anaesthetized, as the necessary price of imagining a realm of *possibilities*, a present or future order, in which the reality of suffering might be received: received, and perhaps diminished and absorbed.

If we allow ourselves to even imagine its being so absorbed, have we seriously kept faith with the reality? Ivan says no. "Choose ye this day. . . ." This is the antinomy which confronts us.

7. The Tyger and the Lamb

It is apparent by now that the problem of evil, so called, is in fact a complex of problems. We have seen that the original religious tradition tended to stress the issue of moral evil, namely sin, but that by the time of German idealism the issue of natural evil had come into prominence in its own right. In the present, postmodern period we have reason to know that the problem cannot be confined to either of these dimensions. Indeed we have seen that both dimensions must be kept in view, not only for the sake of comprehensiveness but in order to preserve the problem as a problem at all. Now by way of conclusion I wish to indicate quite briefly something of what the Augustinian formulation can learn from the idealist-integrative position; what that more recent position, in turn, can learn from the tradition; and what implications there may be for theology and psychoanalysis.

The idealists pressed the question Blake asked of the Tyger, that embodiment of natural evil—"Did he smile his work to see? / Did he who made the Lamb make thee?" In so doing they successfully identified and indicted a covert tendency within the Augustinian formulation, namely a stubborn determination to insulate God from any direct involvement in, and responsibility for, the ills inherent in creation. This common tendency seeks support in an implicit understanding of God as "impassible," i.e., above all passion and change, a notion derived from the Platonic metaphysic to which Augustine was so indebted. What is remarkable, however, is that this image of disengaged deity is at odds not only with contemporary sensibility but also with the primary language of Israel's own testimony and worship. It is not the God of Plato who speaks through the prophet Hosea:

> My heart recoils within me,
>   my compassion grows warm and tender.
> I will not execute my fierce anger,
>   I will not again destroy Ephraim;
> for I am God and not man,

> the Holy One in your midst,
> and I will not come to destroy.   (Hosea 11:8–9)

Here what distinguishes God from humankind is not changeless perfection but precisely the capacity for compassion and forgiveness! That the Augustinian theology must be fundamentally rethought in order to witness to this compassionate involvement is a requirement the full consequences of which have dawned only recently upon the theologians; and even then it might not have dawned clearly without the challenge of idealism. Some have argued that a necessary consequence of such involvement is the notion of a finite God; but that proposal still confines us to the world from which the problem arose, the world of metaphysics. God's involvement as portrayed in Scripture is a function of compassionate choice, not metaphysical necessity; and thus a more promising course, to my mind, is that developed by Jürgen Moltmann in *The Crucified God*.[44] Moltmann recalls Elie Wiesel's powerful account of an execution at Auschwitz.

> The SS hanged two Jewish men and a youth in front of the whole camp. The men died quickly, but the death throes of the youth lasted for half an hour. "Where is God? Where is he?" someone asked behind me. As the youth still hung in torment in the noose after a long time, I heard the man call again, "Where is God now?" And I heard a voice in myself answer: "Where is he? He is here. He is hanging there on the gallows. . . ."

God is there or nowhere. The implication in Christian terms is a radically Trinitarian theology in which God the Father fully participates in the suffering of God the Son.[45] Which is roughly to say that God is present as the One who is free and yet, in this very freedom, most radically involved. But it must further be said that the coming of Christ was occasioned not simply by human sin, as is conventionally portrayed, but also by the antecedent fact of natural evil. The Incarnation would then be relieved of any air of being an afterthought, to be appreciated as the sacrament of God's abiding sharing in the realization and in the suffering of creation. And God in turn would be understood as One whose engagement with suffering dates from the moment of creation: the moment when in Blake's words, "the stars threw down their spears, / And water'd heaven with their tears." It might then be possible to recognize God as present, and present to suffering, in the very fact of the creation's freedom and existence.

But if the Augustinian formulation must be rethought to be truer to its

---

[44] Jürgen Moltmann, *The Crucified God* (New York: Harper and Row, 1974), pp.273–74.
[45] Cf. two very able discussions in a more popular vein: Arthur C. McGill, *Suffering: A Test of Theological Method* (Philadelphia: Geneva Press, 1968); Robert F. Capon, *The Third Peacock: The Goodness of God and the Badness of the World* (Garden City, NY: Image Books, Doubleday & Co., 1971).

own tradition, the idealist position for its part has blind spots of its own. On one level the idealists are to be credited with having advanced our understanding not only of natural evil but of moral evil as well. They were eminently adept at dissecting self-delusion; the Hegelian concept of unhappy consciousness stands behind Sartre's indictment of bad faith and, to some extent, Freud's understanding of repression. At another level, however, the idealists were profoundly wedded to the modern concept of human autonomy. This concept they developed with subtlety, pressing far beyond the simplistic notions of the Enlightenment; the various prima facie notions of autonomy were vigorously critiqued—but only in order that, in the end, autonomy of a more thoroughgoing sort might be secured. The effect of this precommitment was, as Reinhold Niebuhr has observed, to render idealism unreceptive to the challenge posed to human autonomy by the traditional doctrine of sin.[46]

Now the short answer to such observations has commonly been, "so much the worse for the traditional doctrine of sin." But I wish to argue what will no doubt seem paradoxical, that an understanding of sin, and of the radicality of sin, may stand in the closest relationship to the effort to understand innocence as well. And if the Tyger has come to light as the unavowed problem for Augustine, the Lamb, I believe, may be a similarly difficult reality for the thought of Jung, Tillich and Hegel. For remember that in the logic of the idealist-integrative position the concept of innocence is inherently confining; Tillich calls it a "non-actualized potentiality."[47] That limitation is reckoned as negative, it is something to be overcome; that is why innocence for this mode of thought cannot be an unambiguous good. Consider now, in contrast to this position, the image of innocence presented in the tradition. Surely of all things in Eden, God's prohibition would seem to be a negative constraint. But Paul Ricoeur finds a different understanding in the biblical account:

> For an innocent freedom, this limitation would not be felt as an interdiction; but we no longer know what that primordial author-ity, contemporaneous with the birth of finite freedom, is; in particu-lar, we no longer know what a *limit* that does not repress, but orients and guards freedom, could be like; we no longer have access to that creative limit. We are acquainted only with the limit that constrains; authority becomes interdiction under the regime of fal-len freedom.[48]

The therapeutic process may be described as an effort to recognize and claim certain limits as being in fact creative, and to overcome our stubborn resistance

---

[46] Niebuhr, *Nature and Destiny of Man,* 1:112–22.
[47] Tillich, *Systematic Theology,* 2:33.
[48] Ricoeur, *Symbolism of Evil,* p. 250.

to that recognition. Ricoeur is propounding an analogous point in more radical form, as true of the entirety of our existence. Three observations are of particular importance. First, the traditional position on Ricoeur's account differs markedly from the idealist-integrative position as set forth by Tillich. Innocence is an unambiguous good. It does not need to be relinquished for the sake of some allegedly greater good. And this is because goodness is conceived in *positive* relation to God's own freedom, to the "primordial authority," and not in self-assertion over against it. All this is implied by the notion of creative limit.

Secondly and at a second level, the tradition acknowledges the notion of creative limit as applying to the tradition's own capacity—or incapacity—to give content to the concept of innocence. In Ricoeur's words, "innocence here plays the role of the Kantian thing-in-itself: it is thought to the extent of being posited, but it is not known."[49] At this crucial juncture the tradition displays a remarkable sophistication, a sort of positive agnosticism. The concept of creative limit is itself a limit concept. Moreover, one needn't look far in order to find the reason for this reserve; it is grounded in the tradition's awareness that it itself stands east of Eden, after the Fall, "under the regime of fallen freedom." That is to say, it is because we ourselves participate in the common human rebellion that we cannot conceive of "primordial authority" as being gracious. It is because we are tenaciously sinful that we give no positive content to "a limit that does not repress, but orients and guards freedom." It is because there is no good in us that the creative limit remains for us so empty.[50]

And yet—this is the third observation—while sin does keep the concept empty, it may also be because of sin, or because of the confession of sin, that the tradition has the concept at all. The crucial move here is indeed that of confession, the avowal of moral evil. As we noted at the outset, it is a gratuitous act; it is by no means self-explanatory. But when such confession does occur, it is as if one also by contrast cleared a space—however distant, empty and by one's own strength unattainable—in which innocence might abide. Moreover it may be that precisely by positing this limit concept of innocence, without which evil is not perceived as being a problem, the believer enters into the reality of the problem, at the point where God is most engaged. Much could be said at this juncture about the logic of religious spirituality; and much of the best has already been said by such writers as de Caussade and Bernanos.[51] Finally and most tentatively it may be suggested that the converse might also be true. It may be that those who do perceive evil

---

[49] Ibid.

[50] Cf. Jacques Ellul, *Hope in Time of Abandonment,* trans. C. Edward Hopkin (New York: Seabury Press, 1973), pp. 89–97.

[51] J.-P. de Caussade, *Self-Abandonment to Divine Providence,* trans. Algar Thorold (Glasgow: Collins, Fontana Library of Theology and Philosophy, 1933). George Bernanos, *The Diary of a Country Priest,* trans. Pamela Morris (New York: Macmillan, 1937). See also John Chapman, *Spiritual Letters* (London: Sheed and Ward, 1935).

as a problem in its own right, and not simply as the frustration of their own ambitions, may already implicitly participate in a similar spiritual logic. They too may already be at grips with the notion of creative limit and they may be positing, without claiming, the gift of innocence.[52]

However that may be, we are now able to better understand the idealist-integrative position's blindspot. What it lacks is precisely such reticence. It finds itself impelled to spell out the content of the first Tillichian moment as well as the third, in order to accomplish its end of resolving the problem of evil. And so it does accomplish its end; but at the price of dismantling the problem. The idealist-integrative attitude is dramatically reflected in its handling of the tradition. The tendency is to demythologize, to translate it all and to do so without remainder. The tendency is to resist the notion that the symbols of the tradition may continue to say more than one can rationally articulate. Which is to say that the idealist-integrative position is disinclined to acknowledge the tradition itself as being a creative limit.[53]

In light of these reflections it is possible to take one further step. It is a large step, as it entails some very sweeping generalizations. Let us call them hypotheses. Lovejoy observes that the original Platonic conception of God was highly paradoxical. God was perfect in the sense of being self-contained, self-sufficient; yet at the same time God was also perfect in the sense of being generous, going out from God's self, giving reality and goodness to the world.[54] It may be that already in Plato this paradox was held together by a certain sense of creative limit, a sense that the good which God bestows is a function of God's very otherness. Lovejoy himself quotes C. E. M. Joad: "Like Goodness and Beauty, Deity, if Deity exists, must be a nonhuman value, whose significance consists in His very unlikeness to the life that aspires to Him."[55] The imperfect world, in being drawn to such perfection, is moved not simply by need but by what Augustine was to call *caritas*, love: a measure of selfless delight and adoration. To this Greek conception was added the more personalistic Christian understanding of a God who creates freely, out of nothing, giving to the created order its own appropriate freedom and autonomy; entering into covenant with humankind; and ransoming the creation when the covenant was broken and freedom lost. The Christian theme of freedom, quite arguably, informs the best of Augustine's thought, and specifically his treatment of evil.[56] The results of the wedding of these two conceptions of God were sometimes unfortunate, as in the notion of the

---

[52] One cannot help but think, in such a context, of the spiritual odyssey of Simone Weil; see *Waiting for God*, trans. Emma Craufurd (New York: Putnam, 1951).

[53] Cf. Ricoeur, *Conflict of Interpretations,* pp. 397–401.

[54] Lovejoy, *Great Chain of Being,* pp. 43–49.

[55] C. E. M. Joad, *Philosophical Aspects of Modern Science* (London: Allen & Unwin, 1932), pp. 331–32, quoted in Lovejoy, *Great Chain of Being,* p. 44. Cf. Simone Weil, *The Simone Weil Reader,* ed. George A. Panichas (New York: David McKay, 1977), pp. 350–62.

[56] Ricoeur, *Conflict of Interpretations*, pp. 301–2.

divine "impassibility." But the marriage succeeded in producing a powerful structure of thought and an equally powerful spirituality which has nourished Western culture in many unspoken ways.

We have seen that in the Enlightenment those structures were emphatically reaffirmed, but without the supportive religious context. This happened under the sponsorship of a notion of human autonomy which was itself in part of Judaeo-Christian origins.[57] But could the structures long survive, could they retain any plausibility, without an attendant sense of creative limit? Could the sense of limit itself endure uninformed by a spiritual practice? By the time of German idealism the inherited structure had sprung apart. Under the pressure of an ever-increasing insistence on human autonomy, the problem of evil itself became transformed. Attention shifted from moral to natural evil, which was increasingly construed as that which stands in the way of the quest for autonomy.[58] Exploring this reformulated problem, the idealists exposed a lacuna in the traditional theology, an instance of bad faith occasioned by the marriage to Greek metaphysics. To the idealists this seemed reason enough to dismantle the originative Platonic paradox. As Lovejoy observes, this conceptual revolution became deliberate in F. W. J. Schelling—who was a major influence upon Tillich. The fullness of God could no longer be recognized as present in the first, originative moment; rather it must be reserved for the *final* moment, as the sum result—and justification—of the cosmic creative process.[59] This process of productive struggle we recognize as the idealist response to the problem of evil, in which "spirit," variously conceived, surmounts the resistances of "nature." But "nature" in this scheme is precisely the vestige of the once-powerful conception of creative limit: it is that which limits spirit— momentarily—thus inciting it to ever-greater creativity. But now the limit is but a moment within a larger process; it is no longer a genuine limit. Indeed the creative limit, insofar as it does persist, *becomes functionally indistinguishable from natural evil.*

Postmodernity may thus be conceived as an effort to regain, in the wake of idealism, and without relinquishing the idealist insights, a more authentic sense of creative limit. Existentialism is a chastened idealism which has surrendered the "momentarily": spirit continues to struggle but does not surmount. The price paid is to isolate, and by isolation to magnify, the idealist's tragic vision. Observers have puzzled over the existentialist's capacity to pay so high a price and yet believe the struggle to be its own justification. But the position has a powerful integrity as the reaffirmation, without benefit of theology, of the notion of creative limit. In existentialism

---

[57] Cf. Friedrich Gogarten, *Der Mensch zwischen Gott und Welt* (Stuttgart: Friedrich Vorwerk Verlag, 1953).

[58] Cf. Adorno, *Negative Dialectics*, pp. 20–23.

[59] Lovejoy, *Great Chain of Being*, pp. 322–23.

one finds, perhaps, an extreme form of the tradition's own theological reticence. In contrast, the integrative alternative seeks a less radical course, in the hope that it may prove more creative. But here too there is the quest for creative limit, which is regained, on this view, by a repristinization of the earlier religious worldview. But the notions of autonomy which this position critiques tend to be the more simplistic notions of the Enlightenment; and the religious concepts are reinterpreted to comport with the abiding idealist framework. As a result the concepts do not really limit and this more catholic course pays its price as well, in a series of conceptual anomalies which it has been our task to uncover.

That task we have now completed, insofar as we are presently able. The one question which remains is where one goes from here. What are the implications for theology and psychoanalysis? Perhaps I may be permitted a final quotation. In a sensitive essay Norbert Schiffers remarks of those who have suffered that

> they know from personal experience that their suffering and its traces are exclusively their own. They are not universally valid. Others cannot experience them in exactly the same way. No theory can be built up on them. Man's will to live and human hope—these are two virtues that can be experienced by all and built up into theories. Each man's suffering is such a unique experience that it is not communicable to others.[60]

Human hope and the will to live—these are the very heartbeat of the idealist-integrative position, the unfailing source of its legitimacy and its appeal. But it has been the burden of the present essay to show that it is not the only position, it is not of itself a sufficient position and it is not necessarily the most compassionate. Of the analytic alternative one must say that while it promises less, it may remember more. And while the memories may often be hard, it is not for that reason the less compassionate. For there is compassion of another sort which grants to the individual the isolation of which Schiffers speaks, while simultaneously embodying in the analyst's presence an unspoken and supportive reality: the forgotten knowledge of creative limit.

The religious tradition too is often regarded as uncompassionate. The accusation of sin seems harshly judgmental; and so it often has been. But confession of sin, as we have seen, can have the effect of positing the limit concept of innocence; and that, in an all-too-knowing world where guilt is everywhere and nowhere, all-pervasive yet indistinguishable, is no mean accomplishment. When compared to the integrative alternative, the tradition must also concede that its position is markedly less tidy. It seems determined

---

[60] Norbert Schiffers, "Suffering in History," in *New Questions on God*, ed. J. B. Metz (New York: Herder and Herder, 1972), p. 44.

to say more than the postmodern proposal, and yet at the same time to say less. It speaks through a strange variety of stories and symbols which point in various directions—and what it says at bottom is that God is with us in our suffering and that somehow, in God's own utterly mysterious way, that suffering is made good. The tradition gives us a God of compassionate presence and transcendent reticence.

But it may just be that such a God corresponds at some profounder level to the problem with which we are confronted. For the problem of evil, it must be stressed, is not just a problem of coping—whether the day-to-day coping of popular religious literature or the cosmic coping of idealist philosophy. For that, human hope and the will to live are an appropriate response, and theories will ever be erected. The further problem is, in the midst of that very hoping and coping, to keep faith with the memory of those who have suffered. At that point Dostoyevsky's dilemma still obtains. And at that point the will to live is not the solution, but in a real sense a part of the problem. This is the neglected truth to be found in religious asceticism, whatever the distortions to which that practice has been exposed. Life is part of the problem because it is life which moves us on and keeps us from lingering long with those who suffer. We stay by the bedside but then we leave, perhaps to congratulate ourselves on being well. And even if we keep vigil to the end, still, when the other is gone, we remain. Memory fades, and we may know the guilt of the survivor.

It is life itself which poses the dilemma. To go on living we must to some extent forget. To remember with vehemence is finally morbid. Only God's life is great enough to retain the reality of suffering without loss.